1. Reading the Bible

Reading
the
Bible

reading the
Bible

A Guide to the
Word of God
for Everyone

J. Kingsley Dalpadado, OMI

ST. PAUL EDITIONS

NIHIL OBSTAT:
  Reverend Peter J. Kearney
  Censor Deputatus

IMPRIMATUR:
  ✠ Patrick Cardinal O'Boyle
  Apostolic Administrator
  Archdiocese of Washington
  March 29, 1973

Acknowledgements

The author wishes to acknowledge with pleasure
his debt of gratitude to all those who have helped
in the production of this work,
in particular, his Oblate confreres
at the Oblate College in Washington, D.C.,
and Mr. Joseph Wagner of Rockville, Maryland.

Library of Congress Catalogue Card Number: 73-86208

Copyright © 1973, Daughters of St. Paul
Printed by the Daughters of St. Paul
50 St. Paul's Ave., Boston, Ma. 02130

The Daughters of St. Paul are an international religious
congregation serving the Church with the communica-
tions media.

YOUR WORD IS A LAMP TO MY FEET,
A LIGHT ON MY PATH.

Psalm 119:105 (JB)

"Just as from the heavens the
rain and snow come down and do not
return there till they have watered
the earth, making it fertile and
fruitful, giving seed to him who sows
and bread to him who eats, so shall
my word be that goes forth from my
mouth; it shall not return to me void,
but shall do my will, achieving the end
for which I sent it."

(Isaiah 55:10-11)

The Word of God is "alive and active" (Heb. 4:12) and "has power to build you up and to give you your inheritance among all the sanctified" (Ac. 20:32). If this is so, then, in order to get into serious contact with it and consider it for what it really is: God's word which works "in those that believe" (1 Th. 2:13), it is necessary to enter into the dialogue which it means to conduct in an authoritative fashion with every man.

Pope Paul VI (October 8, 1970)

CONTENTS

2. *Reading the Bible*

List of Abbreviations

1. The books of the Bible in alphabetical order of abbreviations.

Ac.	Acts	Lk.	Luke
Am.	Amos	Lm.	Lamentations
Ba.	Baruch	Lv.	Leviticus
1 Ch.	1 Chronicles	1 M.	1 Maccabees
2 Ch.	2 Chronicles	2 M.	2 Maccabees
1 Co.	1 Corinthians	Mi.	Micah
2 Co.	2 Corinthians	Mk.	Mark
Col.	Colossians	Ml.	Malachi
Dn.	Daniel	Mt.	Matthew
Dt.	Deuteronomy	Na.	Nahum
Ep.	Ephesians	Nb.	Numbers
Est.	Esther	Ne.	Nehemiah
Ex.	Exodus	Ob.	Obadiah
Ezk.	Ezekiel	1 P.	1 Peter
Ezr.	Ezra	2 P.	2 Peter
Ga.	Galatians	Ph.	Philippians
Gn.	Genesis	Phm.	Philemon
Hab.	Habakkuk	Pr.	Proverbs
Heb.	Hebrews	Ps.	Psalms
Hg.	Haggai	Qo.	Ecclesiastes (Qoheleth)
Ho.	Hosea		
Is.	Isaiah	Rm.	Romans
Jb.	Job	Rt.	Ruth
Jdt.	Judith	Rv.	Revelation
Jg.	Judges	1 S.	1 Samuel
Jl.	Joel	2 S.	2 Samuel
Jm.	James	Sg.	Song of Songs
Jn.	John	Si.	Ecclesiasticus (Sirach)
1 Jn.	1 John		
2 Jn.	2 John	Tb.	Tobit
3 Jn.	3 John	1 Th.	1 Thessalonians
		2 Th.	2 Thessalonians
Jon.	Jonah	1 Tm.	1 Timothy
Jos.	Joshua	2 Tm.	2 Timothy
Jr.	Jeremiah	Tt.	Titus
Jude	Jude	Ws.	Wisdom
1 K.	1 Kings	Zc.	Zechariah
2 K.	2 Kings	Zp.	Zephaniah

2. Other abbreviations used in this book.

BHP—Biblical Hymns and
    Psalms
  World Library Publica-
  tions, 1970.
FEL — F.E.L. Publications,
    Ltd., Los Angeles.
GELINEAU — The Gelineau
    Psalms
  Gregorian Institute of A-
  merica, Chicago, Illinois.
HYC — Hymnal for Young
    Christians
  F.E.L. Publications, Ltd.
LWH — Locusts and Wild
    Honey, Songs for Cele-
    bration by the Weston
    Priory
  Weston Priory Produc-
  tions, Inc. Weston, Ver-
  mont, 1971.
PMB—Peoples' Mass Book
  World Library of Sacred
  Music, Cincinnati, Ohio.

In reading the Bible, it is important to remember—

The Bible has a theme. Its theme, as St. Paul explains in his letters, is the mystery of Christ, hidden in God from all eternity, prepared for in the history of the chosen people in the Old Testament, and manifested to us in the fullness of time, in the New.

Since there are many books in the Bible, each of which has its own theme, to understand them aright, one must see them in the light of the whole Bible. The same is true of each passage in the books, for the Bible is like "a cathedral where the value of each stone should be judged according to its role in the whole structure."

The Bible is the word of God. As such, it is meant to be lived. Not everything one encounters in life can be analyzed and solved from without, as in mathematics. This is especially true of the Bible. It is "not a problem to be solved, but a mystery to be lived." The more one lives the Word of God, the more one "understands" it, and to that understanding there is no limit.

Bible reading, then, is the work, neither of a day nor of a year, but of a lifetime. God's Word is meant to guide us through life, to which it gives direction and meaning. "Your word is a lamp to my feet, a light on my path" (119:105) (JB).

THE PLAN OF GOD

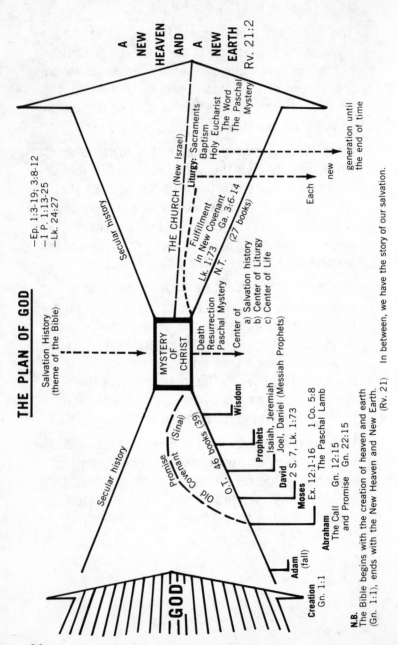

A NEW HEAVEN AND A NEW EARTH Rv. 21:2

Secular history

–Ep. 1:3-19; 3:8-12
–1 P. 1:13-25
–Lk. 24:27

THE CHURCH (New Israel)

Liturgy: Sacraments
Baptism
Holy Eucharist
The Word
The Paschal Mystery

Salvation History
(theme of the Bible)

Fulfillment
in New Covenant
Lk. 1:73
N.T.
(27 books)
Ga. 3:6-14

Each

new

generation until
the end of time

Secular history

MYSTERY OF CHRIST

Death
Resurrection
Paschal Mystery

Center of
a) Salvation history
b) Center of Liturgy
c) Center of Life

Promise (Sinai)
Old Covenant
O.T. 46 books (39)

Wisdom

Prophets
Isaiah, Jeremiah
Joel, Daniel (Messiah Prophets)

David 2 S. 7, Lk. 1:73

1 Co. 5:8
The Paschal Lamb

Moses Ex. 12:1-16 Gn. 12:15
Gn. 22:15

Abraham
The Call
and Promise

Adam (fall)

Creation
Gn. 1:1

GOD

N.B.
The Bible begins with the creation of heaven and earth
(Gn. 1:1), ends with the New Heaven and New Earth.
(Rv. 21) In between, we have the story of our salvation.

22

Learn the Bible Through the Bible

(To be read with reference to the chart)

1. The Bible has a theme.

"For he has made known to us in all wisdom and insight, the mystery of his will, according to his purpose which he set forth in Christ as a plan for the fullness of time, to unite all things in him, things in heaven and things on earth" Ep. 1:9-10).

"He was destined before the foundation of the world but was made manifest at the end of the times for your sake" (1 P. 1:20).

2. The unity of the two Testaments

"The New (Testament) is hidden in the Old, the Old becomes clear in the New" (St. Augustine).

A. The Pentateuch	O.T.	N.T.
Gn. 12:3 22:18	The oath He made to Abraham (blessing to the whole world)	Lk. 1:73; Ga. 3:6-14, 23-29;
Ex. 12:1-49	The Paschal Lamb	1 P. 1:19; 1 Co. 5:6-8; Jn. 19:36; Rv. 5:6ff.
B. "Historical" books		
2 S. 7	Son of David	Lk. 1:33; Ac. 2:30
C. Prophets		
Is. 7	Immanuel	Mt. 1:23
Is. 53	The Suffering Servant	Ac. 8:32-35
Jr. 31:34	The New Covenant	Lk. 22:20; 1 Co. 11:25; Heb. 8:8-13.

23

Jl. 3:1-5	The outpouring of the Spirit on all mankind.	Ac. 2:14f.
Dn. 7	The Son of Man	Mt. 26:64

D. Wisdom books

The book of Job	Innocent Suffering	Calvary
Qoheleth	The emptiness of things temporal	The revelation of eternal life
Pr. 8:22-30 Si. 24:3f. Ws. 7:25-26	The personification of the Wisdom of God	Jn. 1:1-14; Col. 1:15f.

3. The Bible in our life

Salvation "history" is not over. It continues right now and will continue up to the end of time. God calls each of us at every moment toward "the upward call of God in Christ Jesus" (Ph. 3:14). This is particularly true of the Bible. Every Bible reading is an encounter with God, it is a salvific moment. For "the Holy Spirit who speaks through the mouths of the sacred writers is the very same who moves our hearts to seek Him" (Pope Paul VI).

For a **systematic** and meaningful **reading** of the Bible as presented in this book, the following is recommended:

1. The Old Testament

A. The Pentateuch

B. The narratives up to the exile:
   Joshua, Judges, Samuel and Kings.

C. The pre-exilic prophets:
   Amos, Hosea, Micah, Isaiah chs. 1-39, Nahum, Habakkuk, Zephaniah, Jeremiah.

D. The prophets and prophetic books about the time of the exile:
   Ezekiel, Lamentations, Obadiah, Isaiah chs. 40-55.

E. Post-exilic narratives and prophets:
   (1) Chronicles, Ezra-Nehemiah, Haggai, Zechariah, Ruth, Jonah.
   (2) Isaiah 56-66, 24-27, 34 and 35. Baruch, Joel, Malachi.

F. The Wisdom books:
   (1) Job, Qoheleth, Psalms, Song of Songs.
   (2) Proverbs, Sirach, Wisdom of Solomon.

G. Later narratives and prophet Daniel:
   (1) Tobit, Judith, Esther.
   (2) Maccabees and Daniel.

2. The New Testament

A. Mark, Matthew, Luke.

B. The Acts of the Apostles.

C. The "Pauline" epistles:
   (1) Thessalonians
   (2) Galatians and Romans
   (3) Corinthians
   (4) Philippians, Ephesians, Colossians

(5) The pastorals: Timothy and Titus
(6) Hebrews
D. The Catholic epistles:
1 Peter, James, Jude and 2 Peter
E. The Johannine writings:
Gospel of John, 1 John, 2 and 3 John
F. Revelation

BIBLE READING PRAYER

O God, our Father, give us Your Holy Spirit,
make us read Your Word with **faith**
treasure it in our hearts with **hope**
experience it in our lives with **love**
so that we may truly know, love and live
Your divine Word that leads to salvation
through Jesus Christ, Your Son, our Lord.
Amen.

Seat of Wisdom,
pray for us.

GENESIS

The Beginnings

The first five books of the Bible are the books of Genesis, Exodus, Leviticus, Numbers and Deuteronomy. The Hebrew word for these five is "Torah" meaning "the Law" or "teaching." They are also referred to as the **Pentateuch** meaning "Five Scrolls" (in Greek).

The crucial events which dominate these five books and the rest of the Old Testament are the exodus from Egypt and the Covenant of Sinai. Their importance is reflected in almost every page of the Old Testament (Covenant) and underlined especially by the prophets and the psalmists.

From this point of view, the book of Genesis is best read as a prologue, and as a reflection on the earlier origins of this chosen people, seen in the broader perspective of the origin of mankind as a whole and of the world. In this perspective, this first book of the Bible takes on its true significance.

Chs. 1-11 The origin of the world and the pre-history of mankind

12-50 The origin of the people of God: the patriarchal sagas

11:27—25:18 Abraham
25:19—36:43 Isaac and Jacob
37:1—50:26 Joseph and his brothers (the 12 patriarchs of the 12 tribes)

If the book of Genesis speaks to us about the beginnings, it is not merely to satisfy our curiosity. (Science and history could perhaps tell us more.) Rather, they tell us the **why** of things, the deeper meaning of things we see in and around us, both in the world of nature and the world of man; the existence of the created world, the division and separation we find at every level of human existence, and the basic need of mankind for a Savior.

In the
New Testament

In the New Testament we see how the worldwide promises made to Abraham are fulfilled in Christ and in the Church.

Read: Galatians 3:6-14, 23-29.

If you are Christ's then you are Abraham's offspring, heirs according to promise (Ga. 3:29).

In the present salvific moment

We can become spiritual descendants of Abraham by imitating his faith and obedience (cf. Gn. 12-25), and by responding to the call of God in the daily duties of life, both great and small. "It is men of faith who are sons of Abraham" (Ga. 3:9).

Points to think about

1. Note how, in the Bible as a whole, chapters 1-11 of this book form the framework, the backdrop, for the stage-setting of the drama of salvation-history, that begins with the call of Abraham in chapter 12. The chapters can be divided as follows:

1:1—2:4a	The story of creation
2:4b—3:24	The entrance of sin into the world
5	Genealogy from Adam to Noah
6-9	The corruption of mankind
	The flood
	The sons of Noah
10	The table of nations
11:1-9	The tower of Babel
11:10-32	Genealogy from Shem (Noah's son) to Abraham

2. Highlight the lines or passages which underscore the message of chapters 1-11, e.g.,

1:1-2	Creation of all things by God: the absolute power of the transcendant God,

	who acts by the mere power of His word, "God said: let there be light and there was light";
1:26	the special place of man in creation;
1:27	the differentiation of the sexes willed by God;
1:31	the goodness of all that God has made;
2:3	the sabbath rest.

3. Consider the rich spiritual suggestions in places like 1:3, where the first thing created by God is presented as **light.** What we often need most in life is a sense of direction. For this we need light. For in the dark, no one can know where he is going and so we stumble. See the importance given to light in the rest of the Bible: "The Lord is my Light..." (Ps. 27:1), "Your word is a lamp to my feet, a light on my path" (Ps. 119:105) (JB).

"And God saw everything that He had made, and behold, it was very good" (1:31). There is nothing bad about anything that God has created, as long as it is used according to God's will. This is the lesson of the first chapters of the Bible.

4. Has the essential significance of the sabbath-rest in 2:1-3 changed? What is the place of rest and worship in human life? Have we of modern times lost these values? Prayer is the rest of the soul. If men gave prayer its rightful place in their lives, they would experience more peace, joy and stability.

5. Today some claim that intelligent persons should liberate themselves from the notion of sin. With Genesis chapters 2-3 before you, work out the meaning of "sin" according to these chapters. Notice that sin

(1) begins with some kind of distortion of the truth and a suggested distrust of God: "God knows that when you...you will be like God" (3:5);

(2) a desire for moral autonomy: the right to decide for oneself what is right and wrong, good and evil (cf. Roland de Vaux in "La Genese," p. 45). Is this not what many openly want today?

(3) reliance on self rather than on God (see G. Von Rad: "Genesis," p. 87).

(4) sin results in
(a) alienation of man within (sexual disorder),
(b) alienation of man from man (murder),
(c) alienation of nation from nation (Babel).

6. To convey the truths presented in these chapters, the author uses the language and stories familiar to the readers of his time as the Akkadian creation epic "Enuma Elish" (early second millennium), the Gilgamesh epic (about 2000 B.C.) about the "tree of life" and the serpent, Egyptian creation texts (24th century B.C.), etc.[1]

7. Note also how chapters 12-50 are of a different literary form. They are usually called folklore or sagas. Although they cannot be put in the same category as modern history books, these patriarchal sagas, whatever the historical veracity of minor details, are very ancient and, possibly, based on a solid nucleus of historical fact. Archaeological evidence shows that, instead of reflecting the circumstances of a later period, they rather fit in the age of which they speak.

8. In the Easter liturgy, the Church reminds us how, through the Paschal Mystery, namely the death and resurrection of Christ, God has fulfilled the promise made to Abraham, that he would become the father of all believers. Reflect on this and pray for the grace to respond joyfully to the call to this new life of grace you received in Baptism.

Selections   (suitable for a group meeting)

1:1—2:4 Creation: all that we are and all that we have are God's gift to us.

1. See J.B. Pritchard, **Ancient Near Eastern Texts** (Princeton University Press, 1955).

3:1-15	Sin: man's alienation from God
4:1-8	The consequence of sin: alienation of brother from brother
6:1-12	The increasing alienation of all mankind from God
11:1-9	The alienation of nation from nation
12:1-9	God makes a new beginning: the call of Abraham and the promise

Prayer: Recite the canticle of Zechariah (Lk. 1:68-79). "...the oath which he swore to our father, Abraham."

Song: All the earth proclaim the Lord. Lucien Deiss. (PMB - 141)

Thought for the Day: "...and by your descendants shall all the nations of the earth bless themselves, because you have obeyed my voice" (Gn. 22:18).

EXODUS

The People of God become a nation

"And the Lord brought us out of Egypt..." (Dt. 26:8).

The book of Exodus narrates the story of the Hebrews "going out" of the slavery in Egypt to seek God's promised land. As was noted above, this event of the Exodus is at the heart of the history of Israel. It can be compared to the death and resurrection of Christ which, for Christians, is at the center of human history.

1. **The liberation from Egypt,** Chs. 1:1—15:21
   a. Israel in Egypt, Ch. 1:1-22
   b. Early life and call of Moses, Chs. 2:1—7:7
   c. The plagues of Egypt—the passover, Chs. 7:8—13:16
   d. The crossing of the sea of reeds, Chs. 13:17—15:21
2. **Israel in the desert,** Chs. 15:22—18:27
3. **The covenant at Sinai,** Chs. 19:1—24:18
   a. The covenant and the decalogue, Chs. 19:1—20:21
   b. The book of the Covenant, Chs. 20:22—23:33
   c. The covenant ratified, Ch. 24:1-18
4. **Instructions on the building of the sanctuary and on its ministers,** Chs. 25:1—31:18
5. **Israel's apostasy,** the covenant renewed, Chs. 32:1—34:35
6. **The furnishing and the building of the sanctuary,** Chs. 35:1—40:38.

It is significant that many of the prophets, especially those of the period before the Exile (cf. before 587 B.C.), do not even mention the migrations of Abraham as related in Genesis 12. Instead they remind the people that Israel was bound together as a "whole family" by God's act of deliverance from Egypt, and rebuke them for forgetting the great events in which God had made Himself known to them.

34

In the
New Testament

As the exodus from Egypt with the Sinai covenant was the central event of Israel's history, so the idea that a "new and definitive exodus" had been accomplished in Jesus Christ seems to underlie most of the writings of the New Testament, which abound in allusions to events in the Exodus.

Read e.g., 1 Corinthians, 10:1-13.

"...and that rock was Christ."

In our life

In the perspective of the continuity of salvation history the Exodus can be seen as an ever-present reality of the Christian life. Every celebration of the Eucharist is a re-presentation and renewal of the new covenant of this **new** exodus, that is Christian life. In fact, the whole of Christian life can be seen as a passover mystery. Jesus, who is in the glory of the Father, has already entered the promised land, but the Church remains the Pilgrim People of God. "Cleanse out the old leaven that you may be a new lump, as you really are unleavened. For Christ, our paschal lamb, has been sacrificed" (1 Co. 5:7).

Points to think about

1. Highlight lines and passages that underscore the theme of the book, in the selections given below.

2. The original Hebrew for Exodus 3:14, regarding God's name, has been translated in various ways:

The Jerusalem Bible reads: "I am who I am. I am has sent me to you." And the New American Bible: "I am who am. I am has sent me to you." The Rheims-Douay version reads (after the Septuagint and the Vulgate): "I am who am. He who is sent me to you."

In fact, the Hebrew word used here is probably an archaic form of the verb "to be" in the causative form, meaning, "He who causes to be what comes into existence." Thus, it is not without reason that Christian tradition has seen in this narrative a peak of Old Testament revelation.

3. Ex. 20:2 "You shall have no other gods besides me." Name some of the gods that men have made for themselves today.

4. Chapter 24 of the book of Exodus should be carefully read since it recounts the most important event of the entire Old Testament. Compare the institution of the Old Covenant narrated in this chapter with that of the institution of the sacrament of the New Covenant in Luke chapter 22. In the blessing over the cup, Jesus proclaims the establishment of the New Covenant, in His blood (Lk. 22:20). In John, Jesus, the **true** paschal lamb dies at the prescribed hour (cf. Jn. 19:31f.). Paul explains how our whole life is enveloped in this Easter mystery "until he comes..." (1 Co. 11:26). See also Col. 3:1-4; Rm. 6:3-11.

5. Reflect on the importance of the Exodus and the Sinai Covenant in the Pentateuch and in the Old Testament. They form the nucleus of the Old Testament. The book of Genesis carries the story of God's people backward, the other historical books carry it forward. The prophets recall the Covenant and explain its meaning. The wisdom writers develop the theme of the good life prescribed by the law given at Sinai.

6. Read carefully the liturgical service of the Easter vigil and see how it brings out the full meaning of the Exodus event. In this liturgy, the Church calls the Red Sea a symbol of our Baptism and the Hebrews, freed from slavery, a sign of the Christian people. As you reflect on this, pray that every nation may be freed from the slavery of sin and come to a new birth in the Holy Spirit.

Selections

Prayer: Recite Psalms 114 and 115
"When Israel went forth from Egypt...."

Song: This is the day the Lord has made. Lucien Deiss. (BHP - II 68)

Thought for the day: Behold the blood of the Covenant which the Lord has made with you (24:8).

LEVITICUS

A priestly
people

"I will be your God, you shall be my people"
(26:12).

As its name indicates, the book of Leviticus is priestly material. It consists of laws and rites concerning the organization and carrying out of divine worship. They are part of the materials, which have been grouped together around the revelation at Sinai to form the Pentateuch as we have it.

1:1—7:38	Worship
8:1—10:20	The ministry
11:1—15:33	Laws of purification (dedication of national life)
16:1-34	The yearly ritual of atonement
17:1—26:46	The Holiness Code
27:1-34	Appendix

Much of the details of rite and ritual in this book may appear as being of little interest to us of today. Yet, we must not forget that for centuries Israel prayed and lived her life of faith according to the prescriptions we find in this book. Besides, the call to holiness, which is the heart of this book, is a message of perennial significance. "Be holy for I am holy" (Lv. 11:45).

In the
New Testament

The epistle to the Hebrews, particularly in chapter 9, comments on the ritual of sacrifice and feasts that were prescribed for the people of Israel and shows how all these were but a shadow of better things to come with Christ in the New Testament. Read Hebrews, ch. 9.

"... How much more shall the blood of Christ, who through the eternal spirit offered himself without blemish to God, purify your conscience from dead works to serve the living God" (Heb. 9:14).

In our life

The Second Vatican Council in its document on the Church has a whole chapter on the holiness to which all Christians are called.

"This is the will of God, your sanctification" (1 Th. 4:3).

Points to think about

1. Leviticus can be tiresome reading simply because the mass of detailed ritual laws do not interest us today. Yet, what matters is the whole picture. There are five main themes in this book: worship, ministry, the dedication of national life, atonement, and holiness. These can be applied to the present in which we live, e.g., the national day of Thanksgiving needs to be preserved in its authentic meaning. Further, as social crimes continue to increase, one feels the need of a national "day of atonement" like the Jewish "Yom Kippur." See Leviticus 16:1-34.

2. Although much of the material in this book was not written down until after the fall of the nation in 587 B.C., (in fact, Exodus, chapter 20, through Leviticus to Numbers, chapter 10, contains a development of Israelite covenant law through some 700 years, all of it introduced by words such as: "And the Lord said to Moses...") yet, it admittedly does preserve many ancient recollections. It is important to remember that, in the Bible, the period in which a book was written down does not always coincide with or even indicate the age of the traditions it records.

3. As they stand in the Bible, the legal collections in the Pentateuch are as follows:

The book of the Covenant Ex. 21-23 (Period of the Judges)		The Deuteronomic Code Dt. 12-26 (7th century; before Josiah)
	The Decalogue Ex. 20 (early period)	
The Holiness Code Lv. 17-26 (6th century)		Priestly Code Ex. 25-31, Lv. 1-16 Nb. 1-10 (6th to 5th century)

4. When you attend liturgical services, try to see how the readings, prayers, blessings, etc., are all meant to purify and sanctify the "New People of God."

Selections

16:1-16 The yearly atonement: "the mercy seat" (v. 13)

19:1-18 "You shall be holy, for I, the Lord, your God, am holy" (v. 2).

26:3-13 "I will be your God, you shall be my people" (v. 11).

Prayer: Psalm 15.
"...to live on your holy mountain?"

Song: Priestly people, holy people. Lucien Deiss (BHP - I 34)

Thought for the day: "If you walk in my statutes...and do them...I will be your God and you shall be my people" (26:3, 12).

NUMBERS

The second lap
of the journey

"...as at Meribah,...as at Massah in the wilderness."

The rather strange title "Numbers" is from the Septuagint. It could be related to the two censuses of the people recounted in chapters 1 and 26. The Hebrew title is "In the Wilderness." The book narrates the second lap of the Israelites' journey in the desert from Sinai to the borders of Moab and the end of the wandering in the wilderness.

1:1-9—9:14   Organization at Sinai
9:15—19:22   Leaving Sinai
20:1—25:18   In the Wilderness
26—36   The end of the journey

In the present structure of the Pentateuch, the book of Numbers tells us about the organization of the new nation in relation to its mission. The organization was and was to remain a **means** to the realization of the **mission.** This holds true also for the Church today.

In the
New Testament

The wilderness was for the people of God, not only a place of revelation, but also of the trial and failure. And so Numbers has also been called the book of the murmurings of Israel (cf. for instance, 11:1; 20:2f; 21:4-9). The epistle to the Hebrews draws a salutary lesson from this for us of the New Israel, the Church.

Read Hebrews chs. 3 and 4.

"O that today you would hearken to his voice! Harden not your hearts...as in the wilderness" (Ps. 95:7, 8).

In our lives

In this march of the people of God, in spite of difficulties from within and without, God is present all the time; in the Ark, the tent of meeting, the cloud, through Moses. So, too, in the Church today.

So, "let us strive to enter that rest, that no one fall by the same sort of disobedience" (Heb. 4:11).

Points to think about

1. Reflect on the priestly blessing in Nb. 6:22-27. Why don't we use this more often in our daily life?

2. Note how the narrative of the theme of the book really begins in a sense, only at 10:11.

3. What light does 12:1-16 throw on Moses' personality?

4. Look up Israel's journey, on a map, after the departure from Kadesh (10:11ff.).

5. In the light of Psalm 95:10, reflect on the general lesson of the book of Numbers (cf., e.g., Nb. 11:1, 14:2, 16:1, 20:14, 21:5, etc.).

Selections

10:11-12, 33-36	The cloud over the tabernacle
11:1-20	The people murmur. The quails
12:1-16	Moses, the meekest man on earth
20:1-13	The waters of Meribah
24:15-19	The mysterious oracle of Balaam

Prayer: Recite Psalm 95.
    "O that today you would hearken to his voice...."

Song: You are my people, I am your God. Germaine. arr. Roger Nachtwey (HYC. I 26).

Thought for the day: "Harden not your hearts..." (Ps. 95:7).

DEUTERONOMY

The deeper meaning
of Israel's election

"...choose life" (30:19).

The book of Deuteronomy contains a series of exhortations or sermons of Moses to the people before his death, on the threshold of the promised land, after the long wandering in the desert. (The name "deuteronomy" signifies "repetition of the law" or "second lawgiving.") It has been described as an inspired commentary on Israel's history and law.

1-11   Introductory speeches

12-26 The Deuteronomic Code

27-30 Closing speeches

31-34 Conclusion to the Pentateuch

The book of Deuteronomy is a reflection on God's loving care for His people, in spite of the latter's repeated unfaithfulness, and on the meaning of God's law. Its central interest is the spirit of obedience and love that is expected of God's chosen ones. It presents Israel with a clear decision between the way of life and the way of death.

In the
New Testament

The book of Deuteronomy is close to the spirit of the New Testament. According to the evangelists, Matthew and Luke, Jesus, using words from this book, answered the tempter in the desert (cf. Mt. 4:4, 7, 10 and Lk. 4:4, 12). Mark records how, when asked about the most important commandment, Jesus answered by quoting Dt. 6:4-6 (cf. Mk. 12:29-30). John records Jesus' invitation to His disciples to abide in His love by keeping His commandments. Paul shows how the law and the prophets are summed up in the law of love.

Read 1 Co. 13:1-13.

"...the greatest of these is love" (v. 13).

In the present salvific moment

Deuteronomy regards God's will, expressed in the Law, as a source of life. The essence of Christian perfection consists in a pure love of God, since love alone unites us directly to God. The Church's most valuable treasures and her real powerhouses of apostolic energy are souls filled with this pure love of God as manifested in lives like those of Francis of Assisi, Teresa of Avila, and others.

Points to think about

1. As you highlight the impressive lines of this wonderful book, do not forget 6:4-9 and 10:12-13 (the "shema"), the traditional symbol of faith of the Jewish people.

2. Dt. 26:5-10 (the profession of faith prescribed for the harvest festival) is a beautiful summary of the Pentateuch as a whole.

3. What is it that makes Deuteronomy one of the decisive books of the Bible? You will find the answer in Dt. 30:15-20. Compare it with Psalm 1 and Psalm 119.

4. Comparing Deuteronomy with the other four books of the Pentateuch would you agree that this book breathes into the Bible the spirit of prophetic religion? See Jr. 31:31-34 and Jn. 4:23.

5. Would you say that the position occupied by Deuteronomy in the formation of the Bible shows it takes time for man to understand the real significance of God's

Word? So it is in our lives. Spiritual maturity usually comes only with time—we have first to pass through the mill of experience.

Selections

4:1-8	Israel, hearken and obey
6:1-9	The purpose of the Law
10:12-22	Circumcise your heart, v. 16
11:26-32	The choice before Israel
30:15-20	Choose life

Prayer: Psalm 119:33-48
"How I love your law, O Lord!" (v. 97) (NAB)

Song: Of my hands, I give to You, O Lord. Ray Repp. (HYC. I 21.)

Thought for the day: "The Word is very near you; it is in your mouth and in your heart, so that you can do it" (30:14).

Note

1. The literary formation of the Pentateuch (as we know it today)

Many scholars think that the Pentateuch, as we have it today, was not written at one stroke or at one time. Possibly, it gathers together traditions and recollections of different regions and in different epochs. This could, perhaps, explain why one finds, not rarely, the same story repeated twice or thrice (e.g., the 2 accounts of creation in Gn. 1:1—2:4 and Gn. 2:5-25, the 3 stories about the wives of the patriarchs in Gn. 12:10-20, 20:1-18, 26:7-11, etc.). Scholars have succeeded in deciphering and isolating four different traditions:

(1) The **Yahwist** (J)—so called because of the name Jahweh used for God (possibly the oldest).
(2) The **Elohist** (E)—so called because of the word Elohim used for God (a little less old).

(3) The **Deuteronomist** (D) — according to some scholars, an expansion of the covenant renewal recitations. The core of the present book apparently was the "book of the Law" or the "book of the Covenant" upon which King Josiah based his religious reform of 621 B.C. (cf. 2 K 22-23).

(4) The **Priestly Strand** (P)—embodying priestly and levitic traditions.

In the text of the Pentateuch as it is today, the broad locations of these four traditions or sources are, more or less, as follows:

GENESIS		EXODUS		LEVITICUS	NUMBERS		DEUTERONOMY
Chs. 1-11	12-50	1-24	25-40	1-27	1-10	11-36	1-34
P J		J E P		P		J E P	D

Before being put into writing, these traditions possibly went through a long period of oral transmission going back to Moses himself and even pre-Mosaic times. Thus, the Pentateuch is the result of the experience and reflection of a whole people, of God's chosen people.

Put into a rough schema, the literary history of the Pentateuch would look something like this:

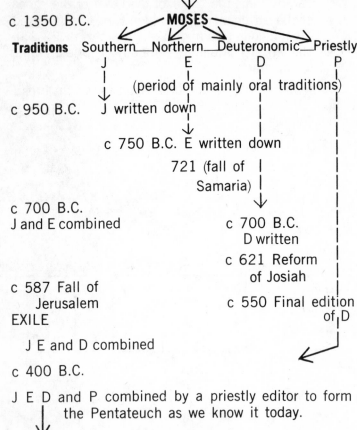

c 1850 B.C.   **ABRAHAM**

Pre-Mosaic oral traditions (and written sources) including ancient stories from Mesopotamia, patriarchal sagas, tribal legends, and early legislation.

c 1350 B.C.   **MOSES**

Traditions Southern Northern Deuteronomic Priestly
             J   E   D   P

(period of mainly oral traditions)

c 950 B.C.   J written down

c 750 B.C. E written down

721 (fall of Samaria)

c 700 B.C.
J and E combined

c 700 B.C.
D written

c 621 Reform of Josiah

c 587 Fall of Jerusalem
EXILE

c 550 Final edition of D

J E and D combined

c 400 B.C.

J E D and P combined by a priestly editor to form the Pentateuch as we know it today.

Pentateuch + Prophets + Writings

Old Testament   +   New Testament

THE BIBLE

What a book you hold in your hands—the Bible! It spans the centuries.

2. Moses and the Pentateuch

Traditionally, the Pentateuch has been called the book of Moses, and correctly so, because Moses is really at the heart of the Pentateuch.[1] As shown in the above chart, the material contained in the four traditions J E D P was not just created out of nothing by later authors. Further, despite the variations of formulation and adaptation, all the codes rest on the same juridical principles flowing mainly from the extraordinary events of the Exodus and Sinai covenant. So Moses could be said to be, in a very real sense, the author of the Pentateuch, and one could distinguish, with Fr. M. J. Lagrange, O.P., between the historical role of Moses and his literary role in the writing of the Pentateuch. While his historical role was valid, his literary role has been conditioned by the theological reflections and worship of the Chosen People amidst the changing circumstances of many centuries.

1. Cf. the Letter of the Pontifical Biblical Commission to Cardinal Suhard, Jan. 16, 1948 (AAS 40, 1948) 45-48.

MY FAVORITE PASSAGES FROM THE PENTATEUCH:

Quiz on the Pentateuch

1. What is the Hebrew name for the "Pentateuch"?

   _____

2. The central event of the Pentateuch, and of the whole Old Testament, is the Exodus and the Sinai Covenant. True or false?

   _____

3. In what chapter of Genesis do we first hear of the call of Abraham?

   _____

4. What was the tenth plague of Egypt?

   _____

5. The real significance of the book of Leviticus in "salvation history" lies—

   a) in its detailed legislation regarding ritual cleanliness.
   b) in the call to holiness for the people of God.
   c) in the ritual of sacrifice.
   Which one?

   _____

6. Name a New Testament book which reads like a commentary on the book of Numbers.

   _____

7. In your opinion, which one of the following words best describes the book of Deuteronomy:

   History, law, commentary

   _____

8. "The Lord bless you and keep you;
   The Lord make his face to shine
   upon you, and be gracious to you;
   The Lord lift up his countenance
   upon you and give you peace."

Name the book of the Pentateuch where
these words are found.

_____

9. "A wandering Aramaean was my
   father; and he went down into Egypt
   and sojourned there, few in number;
   and there he became a nation, great,
   mighty and populous. And the
   Egyptians..."

Where do you find these words in the
Pentateuch?

_____

10. What is the chapter of Exodus that
    records the Covenant sacrifice and
    the Covenant meal?

_____

Answers on page 275.

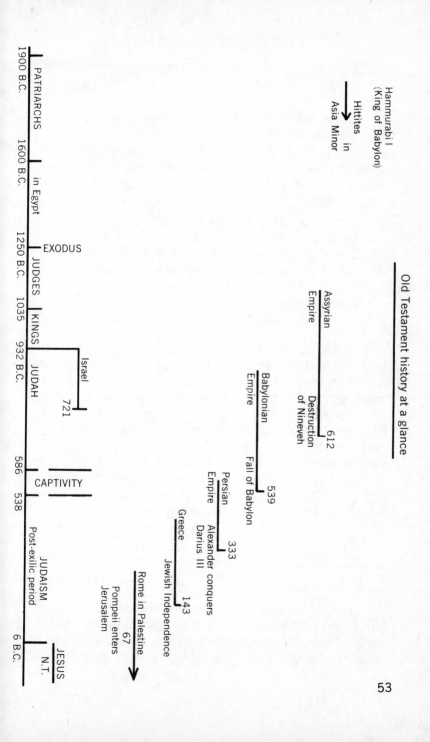

Old Testament history at a glance

1900 B.C.

PATRIARCHS

Hammurabi I
(King of Babylon)

Hittites
in
Asia Minor

1600 B.C.   in Egypt

1250 B.C.   EXODUS

JUDGES

1035   KINGS

Assyrian
Empire

932 B.C.   JUDAH

Israel

721

Destruction
of Nineveh

612

Babylonian
Empire

Fall of Babylon

539

586   CAPTIVITY

Persian
Empire

Alexander conquers
Darius III

333

538

JUDAISM
Post-exilic period

Greece

Jewish Independence

143

Rome in Palestine

Pompeii enters
Jerusalem

67

6 B.C.   JESUS

N.T.

THE BOOK OF JOSHUA

The land
of promise

"...the land which the Lord swore to our fathers to give us" (Dt. 26:3).

The book of Joshua recounts the story of the conquest of Canaan by the Israelite tribes under the leadership of Joshua, and of the subsequent apportionment of the land among the tribes.

1-5	Crossing the Jordan
6-12	Conquest of the land
13-21	Allotment of the land among the tribes
22	Return of the transjordan tribes and building of the altar at the Jordan
23-24	Joshua's last address
	The assembly of the tribes at Schechem

The events spoken of in the book took place sometime about 1225 B.C. But the book did not receive its definitive form till some six centuries later. According to most scholars, the Deuteronomic historian and final editor or editors, had primarily a religious purpose, viz., to present the conquest of Canaan as an episode of salvation history; the intervention of God in favor of His people which called for a response on the part of the people. Hence one need not be surprised at the epic style in which the book is written, a style so different from that of history in the modern sense.

In the
New Testament

The name Jesus, like Joshua, means "God saves" (lit. "Yahweh-liberation"). Just as Joshua led the chosen people into the promised land, so Jesus leads us to heaven. As the New Testament writers explain, the promises to the chosen people have been more wonderfully fulfilled in the Christian's hope of heaven in the definitive liberation in Jesus.

Read Romans 5:1-11.

"Through him...our hope of sharing the glory of God" (v. 2).

In our lives

Through the liturgy, the Church helps us, in a concrete manner, to win the promised land of heaven. For especially in the liturgy of the Word and the Holy Eucharist, we experience in a very real way the saving grace of Jesus.

Points to think about

1. The characteristic style and viewpoint of the sermonic material in the opening chapters of Deuteronomy are found to pervade the books of Joshua, Judges, Samuel and Kings so strikingly that scholars call these books the **Deuteronomist's history.** In these books, the history of Israel, from the end of the Mosaic period to the fall of the nation in 587 B.C. is seen in the Deuteronomist's theological perspective. It is for this reason, too, that these books, which are largely narrative, are classified as the "former prophets" in the Hebrew Bible.

2. The stories of complete destruction of the captured enemy in God's name (cf. Jos. 6:17, 8:26, etc.) present a difficulty to us today. But, as revealed by the Moabite stone (discovered in 1868) this "ban" or "herem" was a religious act, found also among Israel's neighbors, by which the booty was offered to the divinity as a holocaust.

3. The "longest day" of Jos. 10:12-14 should be understood in the context of the epic style of the book. Scholars think that originally Joshua's words could have been a rhetorical appeal for time to secure victory.

Selections

1:1-9	Be careful to keep all the Law (Deuteronomic teaching)
5:13—6:27	The capture of Jericho (a liturgical as well as a military action)
8:30-35	The renewal of the covenant at Schechem
11:15-23	The work of Joshua
24	Israel's vocation set forth once more at Schechem

Prayer: Recite Psalm 105:1-11.
"To you I will give the land of Canaan...."

Song: Hail Redeemer, King Divine, G. J. Elvey. (PMB - 50)

Thought for the day: Be strong, stand firm. God is with you (1:9).

THE BOOK OF JUDGES

The task is yet
to be done

"...that you may dwell in the land which the Lord swore to your fathers..." (Dt. 30:20).

The book of Judges purports to recount the history of Israel from the death of Joshua to the eve of the founding of the monarchy. It presents us with the exploits of a series of "judges," who were really national and local heroes and leaders, sent by God to save the people in their moments of peril and trouble.

1:1—2:5	A transition from the time of Joshua to subsequent events
2:6—3:6	General reflections on the age (cf. book of Deuteronomy
3:7—16:31	The story of "Judges" told in episodes Othneil, (3:7-11); Ehud, (3:12-30); Shamgar, (3:31); Deborah and Barak, (4:1—5:31); Gideon, (6-8); Abimelech, (9), Tola, Jair, (10:1-2, 3-5), Jephtah, (10:6—12:7), Ibzan, Elon, Abdon, (12:8-10, 11-12, 13-15), Samson, (13-16)
17—21	Appendices: difficulties and problems during these times: migrations, crimes, brother wars, the punishment of Benjamin.

The book of Judges underlines the sad lesson of Israel's history, namely, the habitual infidelity of the people to the covenant—a fact that brought with it trouble and suffering from which God had continually to deliver them.

In the
New Testament

The Judges belong to their times. But they also mark a stage in a spiritual history which leads much further on the road to full revelation and salvation in Christ Jesus. In the letter to the Hebrews, they are presented to us as belonging to the "cloud of witnesses" whose memory encourages the Christian to renounce sin and undergo his trials with fortitude.

Read Hebrews 11:1—12:4.

In our lives

A cycle of four periods returns again and again like a refrain throughout the book: 1. the people sin; 2. God punishes them, permitting their oppression; 3. the people repent and cry to God; 4. God raises up a "savior," a "judge" for them; the people are liberated. The people start sinning again. In our lives, is it different?

Points to think about

1. Highlight the lines that underscore the moral lesson of the book.
   a) The importance of fidelity to the covenant
   b) The consequences of infidelity

2. The book of Judges underlines the nearness of the Lord to His people in spite of the latter's infidelity. What reflections could one draw for our modern times from this?

3. According to the chronology of the book, the total number of years of the "Judges" add up to about 400: scholars think that this does not correspond with the actual length of the period. How do you explain this?

Selections

2:6—3:6   The ever-recurring rhythm of events
4 and 5   Deborah and the battle of Esdraelon

13-16   The story of Samson
19:1-30 The crime at Gibeah and the war against
         the Benjaminites

Prayer: Psalm 106.
   We have sinned quite as much as our fathers.

Song: O God, our help in ages past. Isaac Watts. (F.E.L. -53)

Thought for the day: "Time and again he rescued them, but they went on defying him deliberately and plunging deeper into wickedness" (Ps. 106:43) (JB).

THE BOOK OF RUTH

The universality of God's call to salvation

"...that my salvation may reach to the end of the earth" (Is. 49:6).

This little book is one of the literary gems of the Old Testament. It is a gracious and beautiful short story about David's great-grandmother, Ruth, the Moabitess— her coming to Bethlehem and her levirate marriage to Boaz, the Judean.

Ch. 1 Ruth decides to stay with Naomi; her arrival in Bethlehem

Ch. 2 Ruth works in the harvest fields; Boaz's kindness

Ch. 3 Ruth's appeal to Boaz under Naomi's guidance

Ch. 4 Ruth is married to Boaz and becomes David's great-grandmother

This idyllic story, written in the pleasant style of ancient Hebrew narrators, was meant for more than mere entertainment. Like the book of Jonah, it was, in all probability, a protest, under the guise of a winsome story, against the narrow exclusivism in race and religion, resulting from the vigorous reforms of Ezra and Nehemiah. In the spirit of second Isaiah, it emphasizes the universality of God's call to salvation. David, Israel's greatest king, descended partly from a good gentile, Ruth, the Moabitess.

In the New Testament

When the primitive Christian community was faced with its first crisis at the baptism of Cornelius, namely, the problem of admitting non-Jews into the Church, God Himself would intervene through the Holy Spirit to teach this truth witnessed to in the book of Ruth.

Read Acts 10:34-48.

"Truly I perceive that God shows no partiality, but in every nation, anyone who fears him and does what is right is acceptable to him" (v. 35). See also Ac. 17:29, Ga. 3:28, Rm. 3:29, 1 Co. 12:13, Col. 3:11.

In the present salvific moment

Today, history seems to have reached one of its decisive crossroads. One has to choose and the choice is quite explicit; the choice between a narrow exclusivism in race, nationality, etc., and the recognition, in practice, of the common humanity, the common brotherhood of all peoples under the fatherhood of God.

Points to think about

1. As you read, note the passages that bring out the different characteristics of the main actors, in the beautiful drama of Naomi, Ruth, Orphah, Boaz. Highlight some of the significant passages, e.g., Ruth's plea to Naomi (1:16, 17).

2. The greeting of Boaz to his farmhands, "The Lord be with you" (2:4) was a common form of greeting in Biblical times. The Church has made it a familiar refrain in her liturgical prayers.

3. Ruth's plea to Naomi "Entreat me not to leave you ...where you go, I will go" (1:16, 17) still expresses the beauty of human friendship. Compare this with the friendship of David and Jonathan (cf. 2 S. 1:26). As Christians, it is our happiness to know that even death cannot part people who are really united in God.

4. For the "Levirate Law" see Dt. 25:5-10. It pertained to the next of kin—normally a brother of the deceased— to marry the widow, and ensure the family continuity (cf. Ruth 3:9).

5. Although one could find some symbolic significance in the names of Naomi, Orphah and Ruth, etc., the substantial historicity of the book seems to be verified by the genealogy of David given in 1 Ch. 2:9-15 and of David's association with the Moabites, mentioned in passing in 1 S. 22:3-4. See also Mt. 1:3-6, Lk. 3:31-33.

6. For various reasons of style, content, vocabulary, etc., many scholars today assign the redaction (last editing) of the story to post-exilic times, more or less, the same period as the book of Jonah. Apparently, the post-exilic writer adapted for his own use a story which had been handed down through the centuries. In fact, in the Hebrew Bible, the book is placed in the third and final section of the Bible, the "Ketubim" (writings), indicating perhaps its late written composition.

7. Once again, the great lesson of the book of Ruth is that Israel's election does not restrict the universal rule and redemptive sovereignty of God. The election was not based on Israel's right to be pre-eminent over other peoples, but rather on the assignment to her of a unique role in the universal purposes of God (cf. Gn. 12:1-3).

Selections

1:1-19   Naomi, Orphah and Ruth

2:1-23   The harvest field

4:13-22 The great-grandmother of David

Prayer: Psalm 67.
    "May your way be known upon earth."

Song: In Christ, there is no East or West. Harry T. Burleigh. (BCW-19)

Thought for the day: "Where you go, I will go, . . . your people shall be my people" (1:16).

THE BOOKS OF SAMUEL

Son
of David

"If you love Yahweh, your God, and follow his ways..." (Dt. 30:16) (JB).

The two books of Samuel, so called partly because they open on the figure of Samuel, transmit to us a more or less continuous account of the period, leading toward the establishment of the kingdom of Israel. Originally they formed one undivided whole book.

1 S. 1-7   Samuel

1 S. 8-15   Samuel and Saul

1 S. 16–2 S. 1   Saul and David

2 S. 2-20   David as king

2 S. 12-24   Supplementary information

The account of the origins of the monarchy as retained in the Bible marks an important stage in the history of salvation. Before David, Israel had looked forward to a second Moses. From now on, God's people would look for a second David, the anointed of Yahweh, the Messiah. This hope in the Davidic dynasty, based on the oracle of Nathan (cf. 2 S. 7) is reiterated by the prophets down the centuries.

In the
New Testament

The New Testament not only traces the genealogy of Christ from Abraham through David (cf. Mt. 1:17), but often expressly gives Him the Messianic title of Son of David. Jesus, Son of David and Son of God, unites in His own person all the characteristics of the long awaited Messiah.

Read Luke 1:26-35.

"The Lord God will give to him the throne of his father David."

In our lives

Both in the baptismal ceremony and in confirmation, the Christian is anointed with holy chrism. This a-nointing has a deep significance. It reminds him that he is a member of what St. Peter calls "a chosen race, a royal priesthood, a holy nation, God's own people" (1 P. 2:9).

Points to think about

1. Highlight the lines or passages that would help you to draw up for yourself a character sketch of Samuel, Saul, and David.

2. The prophecy of Nathan in 2 S. 7.

Note how this oracle of Nathan stretches beyond Solomon, immediate successor of David (cf., e.g., Is. 7:13f., Mi. 4:14f., Hg. 2:23f., etc.; also Acts 2:30).

3. In religion the temptation is always present to try to make God just a means to one's personal ends, while taking no care to observe God's commandments. How does the story of the capture of the Ark by the Philistines illustrate this? See: 1 S. 1:1-17; 2:12-36; 4:1-22. The books of Samuel and Kings make interesting reading and show how the Bible presents "men of flesh and blood," even in the case of those who, later, became great saints like David, e.g., David's humility. 2 S. 12, 2 S. 15-16, 2 S. 19:16f.; his kindness and magnanimity. 1 S. 24f., 2 S. 1, 2 S. 19.

4. The vicissitudes of David's court and family, as presented to us, have the character of a tragedy. Would you think that David's sin, narrated in chapter 11, had something to do with this?

5. How does the text bring out the progress of David in personal holiness in spite of his moral failure and other difficulties?

6. Everytime you have the privilege of attending a baptismal ceremony and witness the anointing with chrism after the baptism, pray for the grace to live up to your royal dignity as a member of God's holy People.

Selections

1 S. 3:1-21	God calls Samuel
1 S. 10:1-8	The anointing of Saul
1 S. 13:10-15	The rejection of Saul
1 S. 16: 1-13	The anointing of David
2 S. 7:1-29	The promise to David and David's prayer
2 S. 11-12	David's sin and repentance

Prayer: Psalm 132.
Lord, remember David.

Song: There's a wideness in God's mercy. Ian D. Mitchell. (F.E.L.- 6)

Thought for the day: "I have sinned against the Lord" (2 S. 12:13).

THE BOOKS OF KINGS 1 AND 2

The failure
of the monarchy

"But if your heart strays, if you refuse to listen..." (Dt. 30:17) (JB).

These two books (originally one) deal with the latter part of the royal period of Israelite history, viz., from the death of David (around 970 B.C.) to the destruction of Jerusalem and the deportation of the people by Nebuchadnezzar in 587 B.C., the beginning of the Babylonian exile.

1 K. 1-11	The reign of Solomon
1 K. 12—2 K. 17	A parallel account of the two kingdoms
2 K. 18-25	The southern kingdom of Judah down to the Babylonian conquest of Jerusalem

As in many of the other books of the Bible, the author of these two books is not merely writing history as we understand it. Rather, his principal aim is a religious one, to point out that the real cause of the fall of the two kingdoms was the failure of the kings to observe God's laws and keep the moral integrity demanded by the Covenant of Sinai.

In the
New Testament

Stephen's speech before his martyrdom underlines in a very emphatic manner the infidelity of God's people over the centuries.

Read Acts 7:1-53.

In the present salvific moment

The history of the so-called Christian nations of the western world has not been much different from the history of Israel and Judah. Today the situation of the world is disturbed in a way similar to that of the Middle East at the time of the fall of Assyria and the war of Babylon. We may well ask ourselves whether the rise of nations which openly profess atheism does not point to the failure of the "Christian" nations to live up to the basic ideals of Christianity.

Points to think about

1. Note the difference of theme in the books of Samuel and the books of Kings. While in the former, the institution of the monarchy in Israel and the legitimacy of the Davidic dynasty takes prominence, in the latter, the stress is on the infidelity of the kings of Israel to the Covenant, an infidelity that was, according to the author, the cause of the destruction of both the northern and southern kingdoms.

2. The books of Kings give us the general background in which the majority of the prophetic books are situated:

    a. The kingdom of Solomon from 970, construction of the temple

    b. The death of Solomon about 935 and the separation into two kingdoms: Israel in the north and Judah in the south

    c. The end of the kingdom of the north and the deportation of the people of Samaria in 721

    d. The end of the southern kingdom in 597 and the sack of Jerusalem by Nebuchadnezzar

    e. The beginning of the period of the Exile, 587

    f. The prophets Elijah and Elisha in the northern kingdom in the 8th century

    g. Amos and Hosea in the north, Isaiah and Micah in the south about the 8th century

h. Jeremiah and Zephaniah toward the end of the southern kingdom, the latter part of the 6th century and the early part of the 5th

i. Nahum about the time of the destruction of Nineveh in 612 B.C.

j. Habbakkuk about the end of the southern kingdom

k. Ezekiel about the time of the destruction of Jerusalem and during the exile

l. Obadiah after the destruction of Jerusalem but before the destruction of Edom

3. Man's estrangement from God involves the estrangement of man from man (see Gn. chs. 1-11). This is what we are witnessing once again since the rise of modern extreme secularism and atheism.

Selections

1 K. 9:1-5	God's covenant to David renewed (highlight v. 5)
1 K. 11:1-13	Solomon's idolatry and infidelity to the Covenant
2 K. 17:1-23	The fall of Samaria and its cause (highlight vv. 18-20)
2 K. 24:9-20	The fall of Jerusalem (highlight v. 20)

Prayer: Psalm 60.

"O God, you have rejected us, broken our defenses...."

Song: I lift up my eyes to the mountains. Ray Repp. HYC II 70

Thought for the day: Because they forsook the Lord, their God...therefore the Lord has brought all this evil upon them (1 K. 9:9).

BY THE WATERS OF BABYLON

The significance of the exile
for salvation history

For the people of God, the exile of 586 B.C.—538 B.C. was a period of "peak experience." Everything on which they had placed their hopes had crumbled. The temple was no more. Jerusalem was in ruins. The last Davidic King of Judah and his family were subjected to the most humiliating degradation and taken into exile. The People of God ceased to exist as a nation. The mass of the people were deported to a foreign land. Many asked themselves, "Where then is our God?"

But in God's inscrutable plans, this hard blow inaugurated or accentuated important changes in Biblical religion, changes which went a long way to prepare the coming of New Testament times.

The literature following 586 B.C. bears witness to the character of this transformation. The reflection and thought of the books of Deuteronomy, Jeremiah and Ezekiel bore fruit in the golden age of the psalms and the wisdom books in post-exilic times. The writers who represented the Deuteronomic school undertook to revise and edit the whole of Israel's past history (Deuteronomy to Kings) in the light of the teaching of the prophets. The absence of external features of religion, such as the temple, the daily sacrifice, an organized priesthood, etc., led to a new and profound emphasis on personal religion.

On the return from exile, the Jewish people became more like a community organized for the cult—a Church. The books of the Chronicle (Chronicles and Ezra-Nehemiah) present a picture of this "temple-community." The absence of a national authority paved the way for the recognition of the authority of the inspired writings and the gradual fixation of the Canon of the Old Testament. The Torah took on a special importance as a way of life, its teaching being carefully elaborated and interpreted. Israel also saw more clearly its vocation to holiness (Lv.

17-26). Later, this developed in two directions, one of particularism, expressed in books like Esther and Judith, the other of universalism in books like Jonah and Ruth.

With these radical changes both in thought and circumstances, prophecy itself was transformed by a greater emphasis on the divine transcendence, a deeper probing into the perplexities of history and a more ardent hope in the coming of the divine kingdom. It thus gradually developed into the apocalyptic literary form, with Joel, Zechariah and Daniel. Life after death and questions of eschatology took on more importance. Under the stress of the terrible persecution of Maccabean times, it blossomed into the faith in the resurrection (Dn. 12:2; 2 M. 7:9f.). Finally, the Messianic hope revived in this spiritual community in an unprecedented manner (as shown by the Dead Sea Scrolls), thus preparing the way immediately for New Testament times.

THE BOOKS OF CHRONICLES 1 AND 2

A priestly
people

"...shape the purpose of your people's heart and direct their hearts to you" (1 Ch. 29:18) (JB).

The two books of Chronicles (originally a single book) treat, more or less, of the same period as the books of Kings. But they do it from a different point of view, i.e., a special emphasis on the Davidic dynasty and the temple.

1 Ch. 1-9	A series of genealogies from Adam to Saul
1 Ch. 10-29	From Saul to David (David, the initiator of the temple worship)
2 Ch. 1-9	The reign of Solomon; the actual building of the temple
2 Ch. 10-27	First reforms before King Hezekiah
2 Ch. 28-36	The major reforms under Hezekiah and Josiah

These books are the largest historical view ever given to Israel till now. It extends from Adam until the return from the exile. (It is continued in the books of Ezra and Nehemiah, also probably by the same author.) Written about the 3rd century B.C. (much later than the books of Samuel and Kings) by a priestly editor, now called the "Chronicler," they seem to focus our attention on the two sources of Israel's hope, the temple in her midst and the Davidic dynasty, from which the Messiah was to come.

In the
New Testament

As the Chronicler saw it, Israel was meant, in God's plan, to be a people whose whole life was to be a divine service, a liturgy. Peter sees the Church, the New People of God, called to the same spiritual mission.

Read 1 P. 1:1—2:10.

A priestly people, offering spiritual sacrifices.

In our lives

With the exile both the northern and the southern kingdoms ceased to exist. Perhaps this was, in a sense, necessary to make the people understand that the kingdom which God wanted to establish on earth was, paradoxically, not of this world. This conviction that the Chronicler tried to give to the Chosen people after the return from exile is not entirely unrelated to that which we ourselves have to make for ourselves today. As Vatican II pointed out, the work of the Church in the world is not one of triumphalism, but one of service.

Points to think about

1. It is interesting to see how earnestly the Chronicler tries to encircle David's head with a halo. You only have to compare, for example, the story of David in 1 S. 15— 1 K. 2 with 1 Ch. 10-29. Cf. 2 S. 24:1 and 1 Ch. 21:1 with David's deathbed instructions in 1 K. 2:5-9 and 1 Ch. 28-29. This does not mean, however, that his work is entirely a work of fiction. On the contrary, he cites, in addition to the books of Samuel and Kings, other sources he used. Hence his work is as reliable as are the books of Kings, although they have their own approach and emphasis on the positive side of David's character.

2. The basic message of the book for today is the primacy of the religious in human life.

Selections

1 Ch. 17:1-15	God's covenant with David
2 Ch. 7:1-10	The dedication of the temple
2 Ch. 34:14-28	The finding of the book of the law (the great reform of Hezekiah)
2 Ch. 36:14-21	The cause of the captivity and the exile

Prayer: Recite the beautiful prayer of David, 1 Ch. 29:10-15 (NAB).

"Yours, O Lord, are grandeur and power, majesty, splendor, and glory."

Song: Priestly people, holy people. Lucien Deiss. (BHP-I 34)

Thought for the day: "Yours, O Lord, are grandeur and power, majesty, splendor, and glory" (1 Ch. 29:11) (NAB).

EZRA-NEHEMIAH

Return and restoration

"...to fulfill the word of Yahweh, that was spoken through Jeremiah, Yahweh roused the spirit of Cyrus, king of Persia..." (2 Ch. 36:22) (JB).

During the exile of Israel in Babylon, back home in Palestine, the temple and Jerusalem were in ruins. Some of those who had been left behind had even inter-married with pagans. But, after the edict of liberation in 538 B.C., several parties of faithful Jews returned to Jerusalem. Some of these were determined that in spite of it all the people would be faithful to its God-given mission. The two leaders of this movement were Ezra, a priest, and Nehemiah, a civil governor.

Ezr. 1-6   The return from the exile and the re-building of the temple

Ezr. 7—Ne. 13 The organization of the community by Ezra and Nehemiah

This period, pictured in these books of Ezra-Nehemiah, saw in the people of God a refinement in the understanding of their true mission, a slow maturing into a deeper spirituality. One of the results of the exile was that Israel saw herself, once again, more clearly as a people with a mission. From what was left of the Israelite nation, a spiritual community, Judaism, was born.

In the New Testament

Ezra is described as a scribe of early Judaism, a man learned in the Law (cf. Ezr. 7:6,11). The pharisees, too, were a sect praiseworthy in its origins. The behavior, however, of many of the scribes and pharisees in the time of our Lord, is an example of how even good religious movements can degenerate into formalism and even hypocrisy.

Read Mt. 23:1-28.

Woe to you, scribes and pharisees!

In our life

Ezra and Nehemiah carried the reform of the people through a return to fidelity to the Law of Moses. The Second Vatican Council aimed at the rejuvenation of the Christian people through a return to the sources of Christian life: the Gospel and the Holy Spirit.

Points to think about

1. The books of Ezra and Nehemiah are the only Biblical history we have of the Persian period, and even they do not cover more than half the period, that is, from 538 B.C. until about 430 B.C. Originally, they seem to have formed one book, which in its turn, was part of a larger historical work, the first part of which was I and II Chronicles. This artificial division into two books explains, at least in part, the apparent confusion in some details. (These two men, Ezra and Nehemiah, do not seem to have kept their memoirs in strict chronological order.) The important thing is to keep the general picture in mind. The following principal dates about the main events spoken of in the books are worth noting:

B.C. 538   Cyrus, King of Persia allowed the exils to return to Jerusalem, as mentioned in Ezra chs. 1 and 2.

536-520   They think of rebuilding the temple, while celebrating the cult on the site of the temple.

about 520   Urged by the preaching of the prophets Haggai and Zechariah, the work of construction gets under way (Darius, King of

Persia, lends support to the project).
cf. Ezr. 5:1, 6, 17

515   The temple is dedicated and the pasch
           is celebrated (Ezr. 5:19-22).

about 445 Re-construction of the ramparts of Jeru-
           salem by Nehemiah, with permission
           from Persian authorities (cf. Ne. 1-7).

about 430 The great reform of Ezra probably pre-
           pared by the preaching of the prophet
           Malachi.

2. In this background, the book reads as follows:
   (1) Ezr. 1:1—6:22   The return of some exiles
                               and the rebuilding of the
                               temple under Zerub-
                               babel, helped by the
                               preaching of the proph-
                               ets, Haggai and Zecha-
                               riah.
   (2) Ezr. 7—10; Ne. 8—10   The return of another
                               group of exiles under
                               Ezra.
   (3) Ne. 1—7, 11—13   Nehemiah and the build-
                               ing of the city walls
                               (1:1—12:47) could refer
                               to Nehemiah's first pe-
                               riod of activity and (13:1-
                               30) to a second period of
                               activity.

Thus the book as a whole, presents a composite
picture of the Jewish restoration. Nearly a century
after Zerubbabel, who rebuilt the temple, come Ezra
and Nehemiah, the men who were mainly responsible
for this restoration.

3. Ezra has been called the father of Judaism. His three
dominant conceptions were: the chosen race, the
Temple, the Law. However, there was the tendency in

some to assert a narrow isolationism and exclusivism, persisting even to the time of Christ (cf. e.g., Jn. 18:28). This was not in accordance with God's plan of salvation for all mankind. (Remember Gn. 12:3, 22:18, etc.) A reaction manifested itself in two inspired books which appeared about this time: the books of Ruth and Jonah.

4. The time of writing of Ezra-Nehemiah is the same as that of Chronicles, about the 3rd century B.C. But they incorporate documents contemporary with the events recounted.

5. The experience that the Church today has to go through in many countries is not unlike that of the people of God in exile. It could and should have like positive results on the Christians who pass through this.

Selections

Ezra	1:1—2:2	The return of some exiles
	3:1-13	Let us rebuild the temple
	9:1—10:5	The "mixed marriage" problem
Ne.	2	The walls of Jerusalem
	4	The failure of the Samaritan opposition
	8	Judaism is born

Prayer: Recite Ezra 9:5-15.
    "And after all that has come upon us for our evil deeds...."

Song: People of Sion. Neil Blunt (WLSM)

Thought for the day: "Yahweh, God of heaven maintaining covenant and kindness with those who love you..." (Ne. 1:5).

The Hebrew and Greek Canons of the Old Testament

The Hebrew Canon	Additions in the Greek canon
The Law (Torah) 1. Genesis 2. Exodus 3. Leviticus 4. Numbers 5. Deuteronomy	
The Prophets (Nebiim) Former— 6. Joshua 7. Judges 8. Samuel 9. Kings Latter— 10. Isaiah 11. Jeremiah 12. Ezekiel 13. The book of the Twelve (minor prophets)	Baruch
Writings (Kethubim) 14. Psalms 15. Proverbs 16. Job The "Five Rolls" (Megilloth) 17. Song of Songs 18. Ruth 19. Lamentations 20. Qoheleth (Ecclesiastes) 21. Esther 22. Daniel 23. Ezra-Nehemiah 24. Chronicles	Ben Sirach (Ecclesiasticus) Wisdom Tobit Judith 1 Maccabees 2 Maccabees

Note: 1. These 24 books of the Hebrew Canon correspond with the 39 of the Protestant Old Testament by:
   a. Dividing the book of the minor prophets into 12 separate books.
   b. Making 2 books each out of Samuel, Kings and Chronicles. Ezra-Nehemiah is also made 2 books. The Roman Catholic Canon has also the 7 additions of the Greek Septuagint and totals 46 books.
2. The Greek Bible (Septuagint) further assumed a different arrangement from the Hebrew, an arrangement determined by similarity of subject matter as follows: I, Pentateuch; II, History (narratives); III, Poetry and Wisdom; IV, Prophecy. Our English Bibles follow the arrangement of the Greek Bible in general.

Catholic and Protestant Canons
of the Old Testament

Roman Catholic	Protestant
1. The Pentateuch	
1. Genesis	
2. Exodus	
3. Leviticus	
4. Numbers	
5. Deuteronomy	
2. Historical books (Narratives)	
6. Joshua	
7. Judges	
8. Ruth	
9. 1 Samuel	
10. 2 Samuel	
11. 1 Kings	
12. 2 Kings	
13. 1 Chronicles	
14. 2 Chronicles	
15. Ezra	
16. Nehemiah	
17. Tobit	Apocrypha (1) note 1
18. Judith	Apocrypha (2) note 1
19. Esther	
20. 1 Maccabees	Apocrypha (3) note 1
21. 2 Maccabees	Apocrypha (4) note 1
3. Poetry and Wisdom	
22. Job	
23. Psalms	
24. Proverbs	
25. Qoheleth (Ecclesiastes)	
26. Song of Songs	
27. Wisdom of Solomon	Apocrypha (5) note 1
28. Sirach	Apocrypha (6) note 1

4. Prophecy	
29. Isaiah	
30. Jeremiah	
31. Lamentations	
32. Baruch...................	.........Apocrypha (7) note 1
33. Ezekiel	
34. Daniel	
35. Hosea	
36. Joel	
37. Amos	
38. Obadiah	
39. Jonah	
40. Micah	
41. Nahum	
42. Habakkuk	
43. Zephaniah	
44. Haggai	
45. Zechariah	
46. Malachi	

Note:

1. The 7 books which Protestants call Apocrypha, Catholics sometimes call Deutero-Canonicals. The Council of Trent accepted them as inspired.

2. The 2 books, Esther and Daniel, in the Roman Catholic Canon, are larger (following the Greek Bible) than in the Protestant Canon. In the latter, this additional material is presented as apocrypha.

6. Reading the Bible

THE BOOK OF TOBIT

God's presence
in our everyday lives

"When you and Sarah were at prayer..." (12:12) (JB).

The book of Tobit is the life-story of a pious Israelite in a foreign land. Although the book itself was probably written about the 2nd century B.C., the story is about a faithful Jewish family striving to live up to its religious ideals in exile in the land of the Assyrians.

Chs. 1-3   The setting
     4-11   The story
   12-14 The conclusion

Like the books of Judith and Esther, the book of Tobit also possibly belongs to the type of literary form known as Haggadic Midrash. In this type of literary form, the author builds a story, usually around some historical nucleus, event or person, with a view to instruct and edify his readers. Possibly composed as an antidote to the increasing threat of Hellenism, the story of this Jewish family illustrates the high degree of piety which an authentic observance of the Mosaic law was capable of achieving.

In the
New Testament

Tobias is an example of that class of persons in the Old Testament, referred to as the "poor of Jahweh" (the anawim) by the prophets. It is out of such as these that the Church, the New Israel would be formed.

Read Luke 1:5-19.

In the present salvific moment

The message of the book of Tobit is the providential guidance of the lives of the God-fearing righteous amid the varied adversities of this life. It can be devoutly read with profit by a Christian with practically no modification.

Points to think about

1. The book of Tobit is a charming book and one of the most beautiful stories of the Bible. It has to be read to be appreciated: the simple daily life of Tobit and his wife who carry the burdens of others (4:10); the faith of Tobit after the accident which blinded him; the value of prayer by one's self and in the family (cf. Ep. 5:32).

2. Note the angelology of the book, considerably more advanced than the angelology of older books of the Old Testament.

Selections

    2:1-14   The good life of Tobit
    4:14b-19 Tobit's advice to his son

Prayer: Recite the prayer of Tobit (13:1-4, 9-16) (JB). "My soul blesses the Lord...."

Song: My soul is longing for Your peace. Lucien Deiss. (PMB - 161)

Thought for the day: A little with righteousness is better than much with wrongdoing (12:8).

THE BOOK OF JUDITH

By the hands
of a woman

"Your strength does not lie in numbers..." (9:16) (JB).

The book of Judith relates another incident of the almost miraculous deliverance of the people of God by the hands of a woman: the liberation of Bethulia from the besieging army of Holofernes, general-in-chief of Nebuchadnezzar.

1-7 The people of God faced with sure defeat at the hands of an overpowering pagan army
8-16 The defeat of the enemy by the hands of a woman, Judith

Some of the geographical and historical references in the book are incompatible with known facts. Hence, in all probability the book, even though based on some semblance of an historical nucleus, has been freely elaborated for a didactic purpose. It would have been written probably about 150 B.C., possibly to encourage the people of God in their fight against Hellenism and religious persecution.

In the
New Testament

The basic theme of Judith, the certain victory of God over the forces of anti-God, is developed further in the apocalyptic literature of the Old and New Testaments. Read Revelation 20:1-15.

In the present salvific moment

The message of this book, like that of Esther, is that God never abandons His people. He may permit trials, but always answers prayers made with confidence and intervenes, sometimes making use of even the weakest of human instruments available.

Points to think about

1. Judith is otherwise unknown in the history of Israel. Her name signifies "Jewess" and is symbolic of her people.

2. Judith 15:10 has been applied to Mary in Catholic tradition and liturgy. (See also: the Dogmatic Constitution of the Second Vatican Council on the Church, ch. 8, especially nn. 65, 68.)

Selections

9:1-14   The prayer of Judith
13:1-20 The great deliverance

Prayer: Recite the prayer of Judith (16:13-21) (JB). "Lord, you are great, you are glorious."

Song: You are the honor, you are the glory. Lucien Deiss. (BHP - I 23)

Thought for the day:

You are the glory of Jerusalem!
You are the great pride of Israel!
You are the honor of our race! (15:9)

THE BOOK OF ESTHER

One with her people

"Grant me my life and the lives of my people" (7:3) (JB).

This little book possibly contains an episode in the history of a section of the Jewish people who did not return from captivity. The setting is the Persian court of Susa. The people in jeopardy are the deported Jews living among the Persians. The story tells of the deliverance of this people by a Jewish woman, Esther.

Chs. 1-2   The setting of the scene

    3-7   The development of the plot

    8-10   The happy issue and the feast of Purim

    11-16   Additions found in the Greek edition

As with Judith, the author of this book takes an otherwise unrecorded event in the history of Israel and elaborates it for a didactic purpose: to encourage his readers by reminding them about God's loving providence for His people. He may also have wanted to explain in some way the origin of the annual feast of rejoicing, the feast of Purim.

In the New Testament

The message of Esther, God's loving providence over the Chosen People, runs as an undercurrent in the letters of the apostles, especially in times of persecution.

Read 1 P. 5:6-11.

In our times

It is significant how at every crisis in the history of the Church, God has raised up some saint or other churchman, to help the Church overcome that crisis. Let us pray, today, for this intervention, so that the Church may overcome the many difficulties she is experiencing in this period of her history.

Points to think about

1. Esther is read even today in the synagogues on important festivals in the Jewish calendar. On the feast of Purim, in Tel-Aviv, in Israel, pageants on the streets bring the story of Esther alive.

2. If you follow the prayers of the liturgy attentively, you will notice how they often recall to us the thought of God's continued care of His Church, the New People of God.

Selections

2:1-23	Esther, chosen as queen
3:1-15	Haman's plot
7:1-10	Esther's request and deliverance of the Jewish people
9:20-32	The feast of Purim

Prayer: Recite the prayer of Esther in ch. 4 (JB).
"Remember, Lord, reveal yourself in the time of our distress."

Song: O God, our help in ages past. Isaac Watts. (F.E.L. - 53)

Thought for the day: Satisfy us in the morning with Your steadfast love that we may rejoice and be glad all our days (Ps. 90:14).

THE BOOKS OF THE MACCABEES 1 AND 2

Not in a "this-worldly" way

After the death of Alexander the Great, his empire was divided among four of his generals—Ptolemy, Seleucus, Cassander and Lysimachus. At first, Palestine fell to the Ptolemies who ruled the Egyptian section of the former empire of Alexander in a way that was tolerant of the Hebrew religion and the Hebrew way of life. But when in 198 B.C., Palestine was annexed to the Syrian segment of Alexander's empire ruled by the Seleucids (descendants of general Seleucus), the policy became one of enforced cultural and religious conformity to the Greek way of life. This pressure exploded in 168 B.C. under Antiochus Epiphanes IV in the revolt of the Maccabees.

The 1st book of the Maccabees

1:1-64   The situation

2:1-70   Mattathias begins action: resistance

3:1—9:22   The struggle of Judas Maccabeus

9:23—12:53   Jonathan

13:1—16:24   Simon fights to the end

The events narrated in the book of Maccabees advanced God's plan of salvation in a real, though negative, way. The comparatively quick loss of the political prominence and national independence so dearly bought by the Maccabean struggle was a bitter reminder of the oft-repeated lesson of the prophets, that it was not in a this-worldly way that the blessings for all nations promised by God through Abraham would be realized.

In the
New Testament

When in 63 B.C., Jerusalem was conquered by the Roman general Pompey, and Judaea became a Roman province, the time was ripe for the coming of the kingdom that is not of this world.

Read John 18:28-38.

"My kingdom is not of this world."

In the present salvific moment

One of the precious lessons of the book of Maccabees concerns an aspect of the question concerning man's allegiance to the state and to God. There is a distinction between what belongs to Caesar and what belongs to God (cf. Mt. 22:15-22). And there are certain things like the inalienable human right to freedom of worship that cannot be ceded at any cost to the state, however powerful it may be.

The **second book of Maccabees** deals with basically the same subject as the first. Yet it is an independent work, possibly by a different author and from a different point of view.

Chs. 1-2	The author's preface
3:1—10:9	The persecution
10:10—15:40	The resistance of the Maccabees

Even more than the first, this book shows the faith of Israel at this period. Besides, here, perhaps for the first time, belief in the resurrection of the dead is attested, as also the belief in the efficacy of prayer for the dead (cf. 2 M. 7:9, 23; 12:38-45).

In the
New Testament

This belief in the resurrection of the dead attested here and in the book of Daniel (12:2-3) would be more fully developed in the New Testament.

Read 1 Cor. 15.

In the present salvific moment

The victorious way in which the religion of Israel with its pure monotheism confronted Hellenism at a period when other (pagan) religions were crumbling, contains for us a precious lesson of religious conviction and fidelity.

Points to think about

1. These books resume for us the story of the Jewish community that broke off with the books of Ezra and Nehemiah. They cover events of the second century B.C., some time between 175-132 B.C.

2. Man's plans are not always God's plans. Man sometimes would like to establish God's kingdom on earth by the power of the sword, whereas God's way may be very different. It requires a high degree of wisdom to be able to read the signs of the times in order to discern and fall in line with God's will.

3. The long story of the clash of Hellenism and Judaism during the last centuries before the Christian era makes an interesting subject of study. In the New Testament, the apostles succeeded better in impregnating what was best in the Greek and Roman cultures with the Christian kerygma. In modern times, the Church has been faced with a similar task. The Second Vatican Council is a positive response to this new challenge.

Selections

    1 M. 1:1-64   Installation of pagan cults
    1 M. 4:36-60 Purification of the temple and dedication
    2 M. 4:7-20   Jason, the high priest introduces Hellenism
    2 M. 6:18-31 The martyrdom of Eleazar
    2 M. 7:1-42   The martyrdom of the 7 brothers and the hope of the resurrection

Prayer: Psalm 79 (Say this with the persecuted Christians in mind.)
    "O God,...they have defiled your holy temple" (NAB).

Song: Rise up, O men of God: W. Pierson Merrill. (BCW-5)

Thought for the day: "Help us, O God our savior, because of the glory of your name" (Ps. 79:9) (NAB).

MY FAVORITE PASSAGES
FROM THE "HISTORICAL" BOOKS:

Quiz on the "historical" books

1. In the Hebrew Bible, what is the common name given to the books of Joshua, Judges, Samuel, Kings?
2. "...where you go, I will go, and where you lodge, I will lodge; your people shall be my people, and your God, my God." Who said these words, to whom?
3. Who built the temple of Jerusalem? David or Solomon?
4. Where is the so-called "Davidic covenant" mentioned in the books of Samuel?
5. Name the king to whom the prophet Isaiah spoke the words of the "Immanuel prophecy."
6. Jehu was king of Israel or Judah?
7. Who was the last king of Judah?

Mark the correct answer.

8. The prophets Elijah and Elisha prophesied
    1) during the reign of King David.
    2) just before the destruction of Jerusalem.
    3) in the northern kingdom in the 8th century.
9. The captivity in Babylon lasted
    1) from about 587 B.C. till 538 B.C.
    2) 932 B.C. to 752 B.C.
    3) 400 to 333 B.C.

10. "My heart exults in the Lord,
        my horn is exalted in my God.
    I have swallowed up my enemies;
        I rejoice in my victory."
    Who said these words?

Answers on page 275.

The Wisdom Literature of the Bible

In the centuries following the return from exile, literary activity flourished in Israel as never before. The Pentateuch was put into final form about 400 B.C. The writings of the prophets were gathered and edited into complete books, the numerous collections of psalms were brought together to form the book of Psalms (as we know it today). In addition, new inspired books saw the light of day and other old ones were completed.

Like the prophetical books, the wisdom books, too, are not found in the historical order in which they were written. The book of Proverbs contains some of the earliest wisdom of the Hebrews. Then comes Job (about 450 B.C.) which probes the mystery of human suffering. About 250 B.C., Qoheleth reflects on the enigma of human existence. And in the face of the challenge presented by Greek culture, Sirach (about 180 B.C.) and the Wisdom of Solomon (much later about 100-50 B.C.) help the people to hold their own, relying on God.

With the last named, we are on the eve of the New Testament. Eternal life looms large on the horizon. And so, the Wisdom books, too, in their own way, prepared hearts for the coming of Christ, the Wisdom of God.

N.B. (The Song of Songs and the book of Psalms found in the 3rd section of the Hebrew Canon are put in the English Bible among the Wisdom books.)

"Yes, naturally stupid are all men who have not known God, and who, from the good things that are seen, have not been able to discover Him-who-is" (Ws. 13:1) (JB).

THE BOOK OF JOB

The mystery of suffering

"When I waited for light, darkness came" (30:26).

The theme of this exquisite dramatic poem in dialogue form is the problem of human suffering. Traditionally, among the Hebrew people, prosperity and virtue, disaster and vice were supposed to go together. In the development of revelation, the book of Job advances the frontiers of revelation by frankly facing the problem of innocent suffering. It breaks ground for a deeper insight into the mystery of suffering.

Now open your Bible and read:

The Book of Job

Chs. 1-2	The setting of the stage: the testing of Job
3-37	The discussion
38-41	The Lord's answer
42	The epilogue

The story of Job possibly made its way into the Bible at a period when the People of God had already made the experience of Job. The exile meant the loss of all that Israel had already hoped for in a material way. All men too, who suffer and cry like Job can share the thoughts presented in this masterpiece of literature. The inevitable cry is "Why, Lord?" To this question of the human heart, the book of Job, at this stage of revelation, does not give a complete and definitive answer, except the answer of faith: man must learn to adore the divine wisdom of God's providence, even when he does not understand it.

In the
New Testament

The New Testament does not give us a theoretical or speculative solution to the problem of evil. It rather changes the question. Suffering is not a problem to be solved but a mystery to be lived. The Son of God accepts through love of the Father and of mankind to pass through death, the death of the cross. And by His resurrection, He raises us too, giving us the possibility of transforming temporal suffering into eternal joy.

Read Matthew 27:27-50.

"He put his trust in God, now let God rescue him if he wants him" (27:43).

In our life

Job is the man who suffers and does not know why. He represents you, me and everyone. The path of Job is long. One sees him suffer, seek to understand, even dispute with God, who seems to be near in the trials he is going through, yet too far, because He seems to "hide his face" (cf. Job 13:24). Still although the road is long, faith ultimately ends in vision, "I had heard of you by word of mouth, but now my eye has seen you" (42:5) (NAB).

Points to think about

1. The book of Job has been called one of the greatest poems of ancient and modern times. As you read it, try to discern the different solutions urged by Job's friends, and by Elihu and the final answer of the Lord.

1:1—2:13   The testing of Job (the narrative frame-work)

3:2-26   Job's soliloquy

4:1—31:40   The discussion between Job and his friends, Eliphaz, Bildad and Zophar (3 series or cycles of discussions)

32—37	The intrusion of Elihu
38:1—42:6	God's answer and Job's submission
42:7-17	The restoration of Job (the narrative framework)

2. The greater part of the book is in poetic form; in fact, it is the largest Hebrew poem that has survived. The author was undoubtedly a great poet, besides being a learned man and a religious thinker of genius. As you read the text, you can highlight the lines and passages where the poet links truth with beauty. Some examples are: 1:21; 3:3f.; 4:17; 7:1; 8:9; 14:1, 2; 19:21, 25-27; 20:18; 28:18, 28; 38:12-21, etc.

3. Job's lament in Ch. 3 and Chs. 29-31 are particularly beautiful as also the exquisite hymn in praise of Wisdom in Ch. 28 and the description of nature in Chs. 38 and 39.

Represented graphically, the book stands as follows:

Narrative "stagesetting" Chs. 1 and 2

Job's lament 3	Eliphaz	Job	Bildad	Job	Zophar	Job
1st cycle of speeches	4-4	6-7	8	9-10	11	12-14
2nd cycle of speeches	15	16-17	18	19	20	21
3rd cycle of speeches	22	23	24	27 (fragmentary)		

28   Hymn in praise of Wisdom

29-31

32:1—37:24   Elihu's intrusion

38-41   The Lord speaks

40:3-5; 42:2-6 Job's submission

Narrative "finale" 42:7-17'

Note in particular how in 19:25-27, Job's faith, as it were, momentarily defies mortal horizons in his desperate appeal for justice. It prepares us for the more explicit revelation of bodily resurrection in later books, e.g., Daniel 12:2-3, 2 M. 7:9f. (for Hebrew thought, which made no distinction between soul and body, the notion of survival after death, it would seem, implied a physical resurrection). This same desire for survival after death expresses itself in a somewhat different way in the Psalmists, who could not resign themselves to the loss of intimacy with God through death. See, for instance, Ps. 16:10f., 49:15, 73:24. See also Wisdom of Solomon 3:1-4.

5. The day Mahatma Gandhi was assassinated was a dark one for the teeming millions of India. As the ceremony of lowering his ashes into the "sacred" waters of the River Ganges began, passages from the scriptures of different religions were read out for the immense crowd through powerful loudspeakers. The Christian scripture was read last by order of the Hindu governor. The reason given by him was that the Christian scripture was apt to convey the most meaning to the masses of people. It is significant that on this occasion, the eyes and the hearts of millions of Hindus turned for relief, consolation and light, not to some impersonal principle, such as the principle of universal causality, called Karma in Hinduism and Buddhism, but to the cross of Christ.

Selections

3:1-10   May the day perish when I was born
9:14-22   God whom I must sue, is judge as well
14:1-10   Man's short life is full of sorrow
28:12-28 Tell me, where is wisdom to be found

Prayer: Recite Psalm 73
"When my soul was embittered I was stupid...."

Song: Into your hands. Ray Repp. (HYC II-20)

Thought for the day: The Lord gave, the Lord has taken away, blessed be the name of the Lord (1:21).

THE BOOK OF PSALMS

The prayer book
of the Bible

Sing praise to the Lord.

The psalms were used as prayers throughout the history of Israel. And so the psalms contained in the Bible were not written at one time or by a single author. In them, we have the fruit of centuries of prayer and meditation, not only upon the marvels of God's creation and the mystery of life, but also upon the great saving events of God's activity in the history of His people. As the Old Testament can be called the library of chosen people, so the book of psalms can be called the prayer book of the people of God.

Introduction: Psalm I

Book I   2-41
      II   42-72
     III 73-89
     IV 90-106
      V   107-150
(Conclusion: Psalm 150)

The Book of Psalms is pregnant with expressions of the heart's deepest emotions in all vicissitudes of times and ages. Yet in a sense, it is true today that the psalter is like a harp that one needs to learn to play. In other words, one has to learn to pray the psalms. As a prerequisite for this, one has to pay attention to the literary form or type of psalm one is praying, whether it be a hymn, a lamentation, a wisdom psalm and so forth. For instance, when saying a wisdom psalm, one listens to the Holy Spirit rather than speaking to God as in a hymn or thanksgiving psalm.

In the
New Testament

Since the psalter was the prayer book of the Jewish people, our Lord and the apostles prayed the psalms. In fact, there is hardly a page of the New Testament which does not contain some allusion to or quotation from the psalms. The apostolic preaching of the early Church, too, often elaborated themes contained in the psalms.

Read Hebrews Chs. 5-7. (These chapters of the New Testament sound almost like an inspired commentary on Ps. 110.)

In our life

From the earliest times, the Church in her public worship preferred the psalms to other prayers. In the cenacle, the catacombs, the psalms were sung. Throughout her history, in hundreds of monasteries, there was a perennial chant of psalms day and night. Today, thousands of Christians the world over pray the psalms. The prayer book of Israel, the "Chosen People," has spontaneously become the prayer book of the Church, the New People of God.

Points to think about

1. The present psalter is divided as shown above into five books, perhaps, in imitation of the Pentateuch. The last psalm of these concludes with a doxology, which marks the end of each book.

Scholars agree that these are, in turn, a compilation of existing collections as evidenced by the presence of doublets, e.g., 14 and 53.

Note: In numbering the Psalms, the Hebrew and the Septuagint differ.

Hebrew (Protestant Bibles and Recent Catholic Versions)	Septuagint, Latin Vulgate, (Rheims-Douay Version)
1-8	1-8
9	9:1-21
10	9:22-39
11 to 113	10 to 112
114	113:1-8
115	113:9-26
116:1-9	114
116:10-19	115
117 to 146	116 to 145
147:1-11	146
147:12-20	147
148 to 150	148 to 150

2. The literary forms: the analysis of the psalms shows that they exhibit consistent structures which correspond to their subject matter. From this point of view, many psalms fall into two main categories. First there is the "hymn": prayers of praise to God for what He is and what He has done. The second category is the "lament" or "petition" in times of difficulty. These two categories can be subdivided into many kinds of psalms: they could have been, for example, composed for the enthronement of the king (e.g., Ps. 2, 110) or thanks for a victory (Ps. 18) or a battle prayer (Ps. 20); these are called royal psalms. (After the fall of the monarchy, they were retained in the cult because of the Messianic hope in the Davidic dynasty.) In this category, some single out the ones that celebrate the kingship of Jahweh or celebrate the praises of Zion (Zion songs). In the category of "lamentations" or "petitions," in some,

the motive of confidence may be almost the entire song; these are listed as confidence psalms, e.g., Ps. 23. Some are expressions of thanks for favors granted. These fall into a special category called thanksgiving psalms (individual or collective). Still others are in some way akin to the "prophetic preaching." The history of Israel is recalled as a motive for maintaining or restoring fidelity to Jahweh. These are called historical meditations. Still others are evident examples of wisdom discourse: reflections characteristic of the wisdom literature, e.g., Ps. 1, 119, etc.

3. The so-called "imprecatory" or "cursing" psalms present a particular difficulty to moderns. How can they be prayed? Commentators through the centuries have tried various explanations with lesser or greater success. But perhaps the basic point is to understand them in the background in which they were written, viz., the background of the ancient Orient and the Old Testament. In particular, it should be noticed that blessings and curses are nothing unusual through the whole Old Testament (cf. Gn. 3:14 [serpent], 12:3 [Abraham], 27:29, Dt. 28:16 [from breaches of the covenant]; Jr. 20:14f. [for dishonesty in sacrifice], Jb. 3:1f., etc.). In the New Testament we find Paul cursing those who preach another gospel (Ga. 1:8), anyone who does not love the Lord (1 Co. 16:22), as well as the high priest who ordered him to be struck while his case was being heard (Ac. 23:3). Such utterances are not to be understood as the casual explosion of temper but a serious almost ritual invocation for the vindication of divine justice through the suppression of malice. Sometimes it is a protection against the malice of one's enemies.

4. These difficulties should not make us forget the wealth of teaching contained in the book of psalms. It is the Old Testament turned into prayer, a summary of Old Testament beliefs and spirituality. From another point of view, only the entire Old and New Testaments are a sufficient commentary on the psalms. The better

one knows the Old and New Testaments, the more one will appreciate the wealth and beauty of the psalms.

5. In our life, the psalms can be used with profit as morning prayer, evening prayer and in various needs, temporal and spiritual. In this way, this inspired prayer book of the Church will become, in time, our own personal prayer book, too.

6. Go through the 150 Psalms in your Bible, annotating them according to their themes and different literary types as noted below:

H for Hymns; L for Lamentations; C for Psalms of Confidence; Th for Thanksgiving Psalms; R for Royal Psalms; Z for Psalms of Zion; W for Wisdom or Didactic Psalms.

1 (1)	The two ways (W)
2 (2)	The Messianic King (R)
3 (3)	A morning prayer in troubled times (C)
4 (4)	A night prayer (Th)
5 (5)	Another morning prayer: It is God who decides (L)
6 (6)	Plea for mercy in distress (L)
7 (7)	Appeal to God's justice (L)
8 (8)	Creator and creature (H)
9 (9)	Thanks for victory (Th)
10 (9)	An appeal to God against the wicked (L)
11 (10)	Trust in God (C)
12 (11)	Plea for protection (W)
13 (12)	How long, O Lord? (L)
14 (13)	The evil of unbelief (W)
15 (14)	Who may dwell in the house of the Lord? (W)
16 (15)	Joy in the presence of God (C)
17 (16)	Appeal to the divine verdict (L)
18 (17)	Prayer of Thanksgiving (Th)
19 (18)	The heavens above and the law of the Lord (W)
20 (19)	A prayer for the King (R)

135 (134) The Chosen People (H)
136 (135) God's enduring love. Israel's "Te Deum" (H)
137 (136) Homesick for Zion (Z)
138 (137) Prayer answered (Th)
139 (138) The all-knowing and all-powerful God (W)
140 (139) Protection from lying lips (L)
141 (140) Temptation (L)
142 (141) In great distress (L)
143 (142) A penitential prayer (L)
144 (143) Victory from the Lord (R)
145 (144) The Lord, the great and the good (H)
146 (145) Our help is in the Lord (H)
147 (146) The gracious and mighty God (H)
      (147)
148 (148) Let the heavens and the earth praise the Lord (H)
149 (149) Israel's hymn of triumph (H)
150 (150) The great conclusion (H)

Note: The above numbering of the psalms follows the RSV. The numbering in some older Catholic Bibles (following the Vulgate and the Septuagint) is given in parentheses.

Selections

Psalm 8   God's majesty in the universe and man's place in it
Psalm 37:1-11 "Commit your way to the Lord; trust in him, and he will act."
Psalm 92   Sabbath song
Psalm 103   The Lord's goodness to me

Song: Where two or three are gathered. Lucien Deiss. B.H.P. vol. II 67.

Thought for the day: The heavens are telling the glory of God (Ps. 19:1).

THE BOOK OF PROVERBS

That men may know
wisdom and instruction (1:2)

Unlike Job and Qoheleth, the book of Proverbs is not restricted to particular problems but covers a broad conspectus of human affairs and teaches a variety of lessons. It is a collection of "mashals": short reflections on situations in real life.

A. Wisdom Poems: Chs. 1-9, a collection entitled, "the proverbs of Solomon"

B. Wisdom Proverbs:

1. 10:1—22:16   another collection with the same title
2. 22:17—24:22 a collection entitled, "the words of the wise"
3. 24:23-34   a shorter collection with the same title
4. 25-29   a collection entitled, "proverbs of Solomon collected by the men of Hezekiah"
5. Ch. 30   a collection entitled, "the words of Agur the son of Jakeh"
6. 31:1-9   a collection entitled, "the words of Lemuel, king of Massa"

C. An Acrostic. 31:10-31 The good housewife

Although the book of Proverbs is not, as shown by the above, the product of a single author, it represents the oldest phase of Wisdom in Israel extending down to post-exilic times. Yet there is a certain uniformity of perspective. Men are divided into two categories: the wise and the foolish. The wise are not only the intelligent but also and particularly the virtuous and the upright. The wicked, on the contrary, and the impious are counted as the foolish ones.

In the
New Testament

The book of proverbs often places pagan wisdom within the context of revealed religion. Yet the rewards and sanctions do not always transcend this life. Consequently its message may, like the rest of the Old Testament, sometimes need to be completed by the fuller revelation of the New Testament.

Read 1 Co. 1:18—2:16

"Not in lofty words or wisdom" (2:1)

In our life

This book should be read in small doses at a time. A Proverb a day could make quite a difference through the years.

Points to think about

1. The proverb ("mashal" in Hebrew) is a very old and simple literary form. It is the accumulated wisdom of experience crystallized or concentrated, as it were, into a pill or capsule.

The formal structure of a proverb is simple: it usually consists of a distich of parallel lines, sometimes in a series of two distichs, rarely three. Beyond this, it becomes a wisdom poem.

e.g., "Like a gold ring in a swine's snout is a beautiful woman without discretion (11:22) (JB).

or, "a word fitly spoken is like apples of gold in a setting of silver" (25:11) (JB).

2. As you read through the book, you will notice that the collections have not been arranged according to subject matter. But, as you become familiar with the contents you will see that there are certain themes. In one way or another, these themes are concerned with human existence, simple observations about man himself, his environment or just reflection and wonder:

"As one face alongside another face, so differ the hearts of men" (27:19) (JB).

There is wonder at the power of human language for good or evil:

There is one whose rash words are like sword thrusts (12:18) (JB).

Other observations regard the young and the old, women, friends and foes, children, work and possessions:

"Better is a dinner of herbs where love is, than a fatted ox and hatred with it" (15:17) (JB).

Some themes are on justice and injustice in public life, etc. A good deal of attention, however, is devoted to the wisdom of righteousness and the fear of the Lord, which is the beginning and the crown of a life wisely lived.

3. Similar sayings are found in Egyptian books of wisdom like the Instructions of Amen-emope, or the Aram story of Ahikar or the Amarna letters where ancient moralists drew lessons from the simple observation of plants and animals.[1] But the book of Proverbs brings all this "secular" common sense within the perspective of Israel's faith that "the fear of the Lord is the beginning of wisdom": a theme that begins and ends the book.

4. In a remarkable passage 8:1-31, wisdom is represented as absolutely before the visible creation and as having a role to play in the work of creation, thus remotely preparing the doctrine of the pre-existence of the divine Word in the writings of John and Paul in the New Testament.

Selections

1:1-7   The fear of the Lord is the beginning of wisdom

1. See J. B. Pritchard, **Ancient Near Eastern Texts** (Princeton University Press, 1955).

8:22-31   Wisdom was always with God
26:1-16   The fool and the sluggard
31:10-31 The good wife

Prayer: Recite Wisdom of Solomon (9:1-4, 9-11) (JB).

Song: Wisdom has built herself a house. Lucien Deiss.
(PMB - 172)

Thought for the day: The fear of the Lord is the beginning
of knowledge (1:7).

QOHELETH (Ecclesiastes)

The human condition

Vanity of vanities, all is vanity (1:1).

The book of Job shows us that prosperity and virtue, disaster and vice are not necessarily linked with one another. Another wisdom book, Qoheleth, probes the human condition as a whole. He examines concrete situations and shows from experience that even a life filled with every human bliss could still be empty and meaningless in the final analysis.

1:1	Introduction	Theme of the book "All is emptiness"
Part 1	1:1—2:26	The apparent purposelessness of human life in general
	ch. 3	A time for everything, but death ends it all.
	chs. 4-6	Social and political life, labor, religion—what does a man get from it all? Nothing but frustration of desires and hopes.
Part 2	7:1—11:6	Life must be taken as it comes without seeking explanations, for all is chance.
	11:7—12:8	The inevitable onset of old age
Epilogue	12:9-14	Epilogue

At first sight, the book of Qoheleth may appear to some like a diary of an atheistic existentialist. This accounts for the hesitation and disputes regarding its inclusion in the sacred canon, hesitations which were raised even till the end of the first century A.D. Yet, Qoheleth, by his unflinching appraisal of the hard and inescapable realities of life, underlines man's inability to solve by himself the enigma of human existence. In this way, he advanced the development of revelation though in a negative way.

In the
New Testament

In the context of salvation history, Qoneleth can be seen as a cry for the revelation of eternal life, given in the New Testament. It prepared the world to look forward to "what no eye has seen nor ear heard, nor the heart of man has conceived, what God has prepared for them that love Him."

Read 1 Corinthians 2:1-10.

In our life

Existentialist writers often underscore the radical insufficiency of this shifting world. For them, human life is an enigma beyond human ability to solve. The Christian answer based on the Gospels was spelled out for all time by the great Augustine: "Lord, You have made us for Yourself, and our hearts are restless until they rest in You."

Points to think about

1. The first line of the book summarizes the theme of the whole book. The traditional term used is "vanity." The Hebrew original term means "mist," "breath," "shadow," "smoke." In our book, it signifies the illusory nature of this life. Hence, here, it could also be translated as "illusion" or "delusion"; like the distant mirage of water seen by the eyes of a thirsty traveler in the desert, so is the hope that drives on a man who believes he can find full satisfaction in the transitory things of this life, such as pleasures, wealth, etc.

2. Note that the book really ends in 12:8 where Qoheleth concludes as he began. The 12:9-14 is an epilogue added by perhaps a disciple. It gives the whole book a more positive orientation towards God.

3. Note the exquisitely beautiful passage 11:7— 12:7 describing the inevitable onset of old age, which

must necessarily cast a shadow on every human project; "youth, the age of dark hair is vanity."

4. What connection or comparison would you make with the book of Qoheleth and these lines, on the one hand?

"Everything that exists is born without reason, lives on for weakness and dies by mischance," Nausea (Kafka)

and with these quotations, on the other?

(1) "...to come to God, who is all in all..."; "in order to arrive at having pleasure in everything, desire to possess nothing; in order to arrive at knowing everything, desire to know nothing" (the Royal Way of "nada—nada—nada" of John of the Cross).

(2) this prayer of the Hindus from the Gayatri Mantra: "From the unreal, lead me to the Real—from darkness, lead me to light—from death, lead me to immortality—Shanti! Shanti! Shanti!—OM! Shanti! OM!"

(3) "On Me alone let your mind dwell, rouse your soul to enter Me, thenceforth truly in Me you will find your home" (The Bhagavad-Gita. ch. 12:8).

(4) "Behold the universe in the glory of God; and all that lives and moves on earth. Leaving the passing, rejoice in the eternal...."

Selections

1:1-11	All things are wearisome
3:1-8	A season for everything
6:1-12	A man's life passes like a shadow
11:7—12:8	The inevitable old age

Prayer: Psalm 39
Every man is a mere breath!

Song: Joy that knows no end. Gregory Norbert (LWH - 6).

Thought for the day: "Set your mind on the things that are above, not on things that are on earth" (Col. 3:2).

THE CANTICLE OF CANTICLES
(Song of Songs)

"On a dark night, kindled with love..." (St. John of the Cross).

The Song of Songs (or canticle of canticles, after the Vulgate) is unique in the Bible for literary form. It means the most beautiful of songs and its theme is love.

1:1-4	Prologue		
1:5—2:7 A.		1:5-7	the bride
		1:8	chorus
		1:9-11	the bridegroom
		1:12—2:7	the dialogue
2:8—3:5 B.		2:8—3:4	the bride
		3:5	the bridegroom
3:6—5:1 C.		4:1-15	the bridegroom
		4:16	the bride
		5:1	the bridegroom
5:2—6:3 D.		5:2-8	the bride
		5:9	the chorus
		5:10-16	the bride
		6:1	the chorus
		6:2-3	the bride
6:4—8:4 E.		6:4-11	the bridegroom
		7:1	the chorus
		7:2-10	the bridegroom
		7:11—8:3	the bride
		8:4	the bridegroom
8:5-7	The conclusion		

Traditionally, both in Jewish and Christian exegesis, the book has been mainly interpreted as having a symbolic meaning. In this Song of Songs, made of a short prologue and five poems, one can see how the description of human love with its phases of waiting, search, wonder, difficulties, and final union is taken as an image of the relations between Israel and Jahweh, described by the prophets of the Old Testament.

In the
New Testament

The comparison of God's love for His chosen people to the love of husband and wife is extended in the New Testament to the Church, the New People of God.

Read the book of Revelation 21:1-14.

"I saw the holy city...coming down...as beautiful as a bride, all dressed for her husband" (21:2) (JB).

In our life

The writings of Christian mystics, commenting on this book, can help us to appreciate the deeper meaning of this Song of Songs when applied to our spiritual lives. Bernard of Clairvaux wrote 86 sermons on it. John of the Cross incorporates it into his **Ascent of Mount Carmel.** In the last mentioned, the speaker (the soul) is shown as the bride, God as the Beloved of the soul: "I remained, lost in oblivion; my face I reclined on the Beloved. All ceased. And I abandoned myself, leaving my cares forgotten among the lilies."

Points to think about

1. Due to the difficulty involved in its interpretation, hesitations about its inclusion in the Canon were expressed even at the council of Jamnia (about 100 A.D.) and even later through medieval and modern times. In fact, it is difficult to give even a division or summary of the contents without committing oneself to a theory of its interpretation. In its symbolic interpretation, the chorus may represent other nations, or even the rest of creation.

2. As a work of literature, it is of a very high caliber and is dated by modern scholars after the exile c 500 A.D. (The attribution to Solomon, they think, is pseudonymous).

3. Some scholars today express the opinion that, quite simply, the Song of Songs could be taken as a poetic exaltation of the goodness and joy of human love in marriage. But within the context of the Bible, the book is perhaps best understood in the background of salvation history, namely, as a poetic development of the comparison begun by the prophet Hosea describing the covenant relation between God and His people in terms of married love.

Selections

2:10-17   Arise, my love, and come
 5:2-8   I sleep but my heart watches
 8:5-7   Set me as a seal upon your heart

Prayer: Late have I loved You! O beauty so ancient and so new! Late have I loved You! You called and cried to me.... You breathed fragrance upon me.... You touched me, and I have burned for Your peace. When once I shall be united to You with all my being, there shall be no more grief and toil, and my life shall be alive, filled wholly with You (from St. Augustine).

Song: Come now, my Love. Gregory Norbert. (LWH-6)

Thought for the day: My beloved is mine and I am his... until the day breathes and the shadows flee (2:16).

THE WISDOM OF SOLOMON

"...a reflection of the eternal light" (7:26) (JB).

This book was written sometime between 100 and 50 B.C. possibly by an Alexandrian Jew to meet the same problem which occasioned the production of the book of Sirach: the meeting of Greek culture and the Jewish faith.

Chs. 1-5   Wisdom and human destiny: the vital importance of Wisdom

6-9   Origin and nature of Wisdom and the means to acquire it

10-19 A description of divine Wisdom as directing the destiny of Israel throughout history

Like Sirach, the author is addressing himself to his co-religionists who were in danger of being led astray by the brilliance of Greek culture as well as to those non-Jews who felt the attraction of the beauty and nobility of the Jewish monotheist faith. This Wisdom which comes from God and was created before all things found its rest not in the human splendor of Greek culture but only in Israel, in the Temple of Jerusalem and the Law of Moses. It was she who guided Israel's destiny in the past, it is she who guides her in the present.

In the New Testament

The personification of Wisdom began in Proverbs and Sirach, and is here further developed to represent almost a semi-independent power, almost identical with God, in 7:22—8:1. Compare Proverbs 8:22-31, Sirach 24:3-14 and Wisdom 7:22—8:1 with one another and with passages in John and Paul. In this sense, this last book of the Old Testament appears as a bridge between the Old and the New Testaments.

Read 1 Co. 1:24-30 or Jn. 1:1-14.

In our life

This book presents excellent passages for reflection and meditation especially if we take them in connection with the corresponding New Testament passages (cf. below).

Points to think about

1. This book, like Sirach, is not in the Jewish Canon, and therefore not included in the Protestant Bible. It seems to have been directly written in Greek and preserved in the same language.

2. The author uses terms taken from Greek philosophy like "immortality" (e.g., 3:4, 4:1, 8:13, 15:3) or "incorruption." However, caution must be used in understanding what the author means by these terms, because his thinking still remains authentically Hebrew (where the Greek dichotomy of man into body and soul was unknown).

3. From Justin onwards, Christian tradition in its development of the doctrine of the Holy Trinity has almost always seen in the personification of divine Wisdom in 7:22—8:1, the Word, the second person of the Blessed Trinity. It is particularly interesting to note that the images, used by the author in vv. 25-26 to describe the origin of wisdom from God, indicate, at the same time, that she has a share in what she proceeds from. Note also her qualities mentioned later as omnipotence (vv. 23-27), sanctity and immutability (vv. 22-25) —all exclusively divine qualities.

Some comparisons between passages in Wisdom and in some New Testament authors:

(1) Paul: Rm. 1:18-20 and Ws. 13:1-9
               Col. 1:15 and Ws. 7:26
(2) Hebrews: 1:3 and Ws. 7:26
(3) John: 1:1, 18 and Ws. 8:3; 9:4
               1:3, 10 and Ws. 7:21; 8:6; 9:1

Selections

3:1-12   The destiny of the virtuous and that of the wicked

7:25—8:8 Wisdom: a reflection of God

14:12-31 Idolatry and its consequences

Prayer: Recite Wisdom 9:1-11.
"Send her forth from your throne of glory."

Song: All of my life, I will praise the living God. Sr. Mary Grace (HYC-117)

Thought for the day: "With you is Wisdom...send her forth from your throne of glory" (9:9, 10) (JB).

SIRACH (Ecclesiasticus)

"To fear the Lord is the perfection of Wisdom" (1:16) (JB).

Unlike the book of Proverbs, this book is not a compilation of various works, but the product of one man's reflection and meditation on the Mosaic Law and all that it meant to God's people. The author treats of day-to-day problems as well as of profound questions.

Chs. 1-43	Moral lessons for all
44:1—50:21	Praise of Israel's ancestors, who based their lives on the law.
50:22—51:30	Epilogue

From the preface, written by the author's grandson, who also translated the book, we can gather the background of the book. The book was written in Hebrew sometime between 200 and 175 B.C., probably about 180 and translated into Greek about 132 B.C. It was the period when Antiochus III wanted to impose Greek culture on the Jews. Sirach courageously took up the task of writing a book that would be, essentially, an apology for Judaism. He made a synthesis of revealed religion and empirical wisdom with a view of showing to all, Jews and good pagans alike, where true Wisdom came from (cf. 19:20).

In the New Testament

The author, Sirach, seems to have been a sage who lived in Jerusalem and was thoroughly imbued with the love of the Law, the priesthood, the temple and the divine worship. His admiration for the "fear of the Lord" can only be compared with Paul's admiration for charity in the New Testament.

Compare Si. 1:11-25 with 1 Co. 13:1-13.

In our life

For Sirach, to be genuinely religious, meant, not a flight from reality but facing life as it is. Holiness is acquired, not outside of time, but in time. One must have the courage of one's convictions to be able to live up to them, and if necessary, to endure shame and humiliation for one's faith. This was the lesson that Israel needed at the time the author wrote. Is it not what we need today?

Points to think about

1. Like Proverbs, the book is best read in small doses, although our author seems to group his matter better than is the case with Proverbs.

2. This book too, is not in the Hebrew Canon. Perhaps it appeared too late. Hence, it is not in Protestant Bibles. But the Catholic Church has always recognized its canonicity and used it much in her Roman liturgy.

3. In this book, too, as in Proverbs, there is a remarkable passage, where Wisdom is considered as created before all things, and poured out upon all that God made— a passage which remotely prepared the doctrine of the pre-existence of the divine Word as explained by John and Paul. Compare Si. 24:1-30 with Col. 1:14-20, and Jn. 1:1-14.

Selections

    1:11-25 The fear of the Lord
    18:1-14 The greatness of God and the smallness
             of man
    39:1-11 The study of the Law
    44:1-15 The example of holy men of old

Prayer: Recite Sirach 51:1-17.
    "I will give thanks to you, Lord and King..." (JB).

Song: Faith of our fathers. (PMB-188).

Thought for the day: All Wisdom comes from the Lord and is with him forever (Si. 1:1).

MY FAVORITE PASSAGES FROM THE WISDOM BOOKS:

Quiz on the Wisdom books

1. In the Hebrew Bible, under what classification are the Wisdom books found?
2. "The Lord created me at the beginning of his work, the first of his acts of old. Ages ago I was set up, at the first before the beginning of the earth."
   From what book of Wisdom are these words?
3. What is the theme of the book of Job?
4. "You are a priest forever after the order of Melchisedech."
   Which is the psalm that contains these words?
5. The best way of reading the book of Proverbs is to read it
   a) at a stretch
   b) a little at a time
   Mark the right answer.
6. "Until the day breathes and the shadows flee."
   Name the book where these words are found.
7. "Remember also your Creator in the days of your youth, before the evil days come, and the years draw nigh, when you will say, 'I have no pleasure in them.'"
   In which of the Wisdom books are these words found?
8. In what book is the emptiness of mere earthly happiness emphatically underlined?
9. "This is the fate of those who have foolish confidence

   Sheol shall be their home.
   But God will ransom my soul from the power of Sheol, for he will receive me."
   These words are   a) from the book of Job.
                      b) from the book of Psalms.
   Mark correct answer.

10. "For everything there is a season, and a time for every matter under heaven."
    These words are from   a) Proverbs.
                           b) Qoheleth.
    Mark correct answer.

Answers on page 275.

THE PROPHETS

"The Word of the Lord..."

The appearance of the prophets in Israel marks an important stage in salvation history. It was their privilege to deepen the understanding of the spiritual dimensions of the promises and the covenant. They were also the harbingers of Israel's messianic hope, particularly as enunciated in Nathan's oracle to David (2 S. 7). As the exodus with the Sinai Covenant has been called the center of the history of Israel, the prophetic teaching can be called the heart of the Old Testament.

"In many and various ways, God spoke of old to our fathers by the prophets..." (Heb. 1:1).

ISAIAH

The prophet
of God's holiness

"Holy, holy, holy is the Lord of hosts" (6:3).

It was an ominous time with impending catastrophe. The Assyrian threat was becoming daily more and more acute. Samaria was to fall in 721 B.C. Jerusalem would be besieged in 701 B.C. and Judah practically made a vassal of Assyria. Isaiah's prophetic career stretches across this disturbed period (some 40 years).

1-5	Oracles against Israel and Judah (early ministry?)
6	Vision and call
7-11	Immanuel prophecies
12	Psalm
13-23	Against foreign nations
24-27	The "little apocalypse" of Isaiah
28-32	Later oracles of Isaiah
33	Psalm of hope
34-35	The "greater apocalypse" of Isaiah
36-39	Historical appendix

Isaiah is called the prophet of God's holiness. The inaugural vision in 6:1-13 sets the tone to the whole of his life and work, and it is in this light that his teaching is best understood. In the preaching of this great prophet, we see the first faint outlines of the mystery of grace and redemption: God wishes his creature to share in His infinite holiness.

In the
New Testament

Isaiah's laments over the sinful nation and the faithless city, Jerusalem, are very remarkable (cf. 1:4-6, 21-24, etc.). One cannot read these laments without remembering that far down the ages another voice was lifted in sorrow over the same city because she did not recognize the opportunity when God offered it.

Read Luke 13:34-35, 19:41-44.

In the present salvific moment

Some often think of the prophets as men, who fore-told the future. But this is, in a way, incidental to the prophetic vocation. As the etymology of the word it-self implies, the prophet's essential task was to speak to the people in God's name. They were, accordingly, men who in their lives experienced the divine in a remarkable way. Isaiah's particular grace was a deep insight into the awesome holiness of God. We are reminded of this at every holy Mass as we pray: "Holy, holy, holy Lord, God...."

Points to think about

1. To facilitate the reading of Isaiah, Chapters 1-39, note the following:

Vision	To Israel	To other nations	Apocalypses	Hymns	Information
Call of the Prophet. Ch 6	Ch 1-5, 7-11 Early preaching Chs 28-32 Later preaching	Chs 13-23	Chs 24-27 Probably later than Chs 40-66 and Chs 34-35 also possibly late	Ch 12 Date un-certain Ch 33 Uncertain date	Chs 36-39 Mainly from 2 K 18:30— 20:19

2. As you go through the text, highlight the lines or passages where Isaiah underscores the holiness of God and the sinfulness of man. For this, read and meditate on ch 6. Then read chs 1-5 in the light of the main themes of ch 6.

Ch 6 verses

1-4   The vision: Isaiah's realization of God's holiness and greatness

5	Consciousness of his own nothingness and sinfulness (and that of his people)
6-7	The experience of forgiveness
8-9a	The call and the answer
9b-10	The content of his preaching and its negative result
11-12	The punishment=exile
13	The faithful remnant and the Messianic hope

This vision is one of the classic passages of prophetic literature. It should be read in the light of the New Testament experience of forgiveness of sins. Note how verses 6-9a bring out how God, as it were, claims the prophet in this experience. Throughout the rest of the book, we see how Isaiah never lost the peace of God's forgiveness.

3. According to Isaiah what is the relationship between true worship and the moral life? (cf. e.g., 1:1-17)

4. Isaiah's message rings true down the ages: for history is witness to the wreckage and ruin of civilizations that had no place for God or for His moral law (cf. Is. 5:15).

5. The song of the vineyard in 5:1-24 makes a good reflection on what we have done with God's gifts, and what a poor thing we have made of a life blessed with God's mercies.

6. The book of Isaiah, as we have it in the Bible, has 66 chapters. Most scholars are generally agreed that not all this material comes from the 8th century Jerusalem prophet Isaiah. Chs 40-66, although included in the same scroll, are supposed to come from a later period, towards the end of the exile and later. This section is often called "Second Isaiah." (Chs 24-27 and 34-35, too, are supposed to come from a later period, even later than Second Isaiah.)

Selections

1:1-17   The religion that God wants
5:1-7   The song of the vineyard
6:1-13   (God's holiness and man's sinfulness)
          The call of Isaiah
11:1-9   A messianic poem
28:1-17   Oracle against Samaria

Prayer: Isaiah 12:1-6
"...for great in your midst is the Holy One of Israel."

Song: Holy, holy, holy, Lord God Almighty. John B. Dykes. (PMB-184)

Thought for the day: "Great in your midst is the Holy One of Israel" (12:6).

ISAIAH 40-66

A light
to the nations

The scene has changed. The power of Babylon, successor of Assyria, as mistress of the world, is on the wane. Cyrus of Persia is already a leading figure, who will eventually gain control of the Golden Crescent. As noted above, an unknown prophet of the Isian school toward the end of the exile (more than 150 years after Isaiah of Jerusalem) sees in this change of events the hand of Jahweh, the Lord of history, before whom "the nations are like a drop on the pail's rim" (40:15) (JB). There is prophecy and poetry in this section which proclaims the dawn of a new age, an age that would see the fulfillment, in an altogether remarkable way, of the destiny of God's people as a "light to the nations" (49:6).

40-55 The book of consolation of Israel: a new exodus, a new age

56-66 The third section of the book of Isaiah: the conversion of pagans and the glorious resurrection of Jerusalem

All the great ideas of Isaiah of Jerusalem, the master-prophet, are found here. In these chapters, they reach newer heights of poetic elevation and a profounder depth of understanding of God's action in history in the light of the later prophetic tradition, especially, Jeremiah and Ezekiel. It was the intention of Jahweh, the "Holy One of Israel," God of the whole earth (54:5), to accomplish His plan through Israel in spite of everything. Now that the purification of the exile is at an end, there will be a "new Exodus" out of which will emerge a "new Israel," a new Israel bound to Jahweh in a new relationship (54:4-10) and with a "new song" on her lips (42:10-12). But she will accomplish this universal mission, in God's way, not in hers.

This deep mystery of the destiny of God's people and of salvation history finds expression in the mysterious figure of the "Suffering Servant."

In the New Testament

The New Testament writers show how, in Jesus Christ, God brought to fulfillment all the prophecies and the hope of Israel's long history. He was the New Israel in whom the new Exodus, the definite "passover" from slavery to the freedom of the children of God, was accomplished. In Him, the "Servant Songs" of our prophet find their true and full meaning.

Read Acts 8:26-40.

"Beginning with this scripture, he told him the good news of Jesus" (8:35).

In the present salvific moment

The liturgical readings of the feast of the Epiphany bring before us the glorious resurrection of Jerusalem described in ch. 60. "Arise, shine out, for your light has come...." Light and darkness are spiritual symbols. The light of Christ shines as a beacon light in the darkness of the night. It shines out through the surrounding darkness unquenched, but yet not dispersing the darkness (Jn. 1:4, 5).

Today men are invited to the Church, the New Israel, to come forward to this light, and walk in the light so as to escape the darkness around them.

Points to think about

1. Highlight the lines and sections which underscore the major themes of "Second Isaiah": the majesty of God (e.g., 40:12-18); master of history (40:27); the powerlessness of idols (e.g., 44:6-8); the mission of the Servant (See below: Servant Songs); the glorious resurrection of Jerusalem (52:7f.); the new exodus (40:3, 49:10).

2. Can you recognize the main themes of our prophet's message in the "prologue," (40:1-11), and see the rest of the book as a development of these themes?

3. What is the specific contribution of our prophet to the development of revelation on providence? Would you agree with Martin Buber in calling "Second Isaiah," "the originator of a theology of world history"? See, for example, 40:27.

4. The historical background of Is. 40-66 is so different from that of Isaiah 1-39, yet it is not predicted for some time in the future, but is assumed to exist in the time of writing (cf. 44:26, 49:19, 51:3). In addition, a marked difference in literary style, clear even in translations, and a new tone in the theological emphasis, which set these chapters off from the earlier section of Isaiah (ch. 1-39), seem to justify the attribution of these

chapters by scholars to a later prophet of the Isaian "school." For want of a name, the author is called "Deutero-Isaiah" or "Second Isaiah."

5. An important contribution of the prophets in the Old Testament was to help with the inner development of the history of salvation by deepening the understanding of the promises and the covenant. In Deutero-Isaiah, we see that the promise repeatedly made to Abraham, that through him, the whole world would be blessed (cf. Gn. 12:3, 22:18, etc.) is to be realized in a wonderful way, especially through the mysterious Suffering Servant.

6. The main "servant songs" (42:1-9, 49:1-6, 50:4-11, 52:13—53:12) present this mysterious figure of the Servant. The texts, however, seem to refer at times to the servant Israel as a people, e.g., 44:21, and at times, to an individual personal servant who would perfectly fulfill Israel's mission, e.g., 49:5. (It would not be necessary, however, to have to choose between the two, if this Servant includes and represents Israel, the community of the Chosen people.) It would be his task "to gather Israel" (49:5) and redeem many by his sufferings and his death (53:11-12). He will be the light of the nations (49:6).

Exegetes may differ in the identification of this mysterious figure. But they would generally agree that neither Israel taken in a corporate sense nor any single person mentioned in the Old Testament corresponds completely to the figure presented in these texts. The early Christian Church and Patristic exegesis consistently see Christ in this mysterious figure (See Ac. 3:13, 26; 4:27, 30; Lk. 22:37; Mt. 8:17; Mk. 9:12; Rm. 4:25, 15:21; 1 P. 2:21-25, etc.).

The fourth Servant poem (52:13—53:12) is worth careful reading. In it, the theme reaches its climax.

    A. 52:13-15 Yahweh introduces the Servant, announces his final triumph and elevation.

  B. 53:1-3   To the kings of the nations, the whole thing is incredible.

  53:4-6   Their eyes are suddenly opened to see the true meaning of his suffering.

  53:7-9   The way the Servant endured suffering is emphasized.

  C. Conclusion:

  53:10-12 All the preceding are summed up in a grand climax: the glorification of the Servant is announced.

7. The chapters 56-66 seem to presuppose an historical situation somewhat later than that presupposed in chapters 40-55, after the return from exile. They are, however, so similar to chapters 40-55, that some sections of them are attributed to Second Isaiah and other sections to a disciple or disciples of his.

N.B. The style and thought of the poems in chs. 60-62 are so similar to those of chs. 40-55 that scholars think they must have been composed either by the author of the latter or, at least, by one of his immediate disciples. In fact, they form the nucleus of this third section of Isaiah.

8. Chapters 34 and 35, and 24-27 are, in the opinion of scholars, seemingly the latest sections of the book. They see beyond the immediate events toward eschatological times: the final judgment of God.

9. As you read Second Isaiah, reflect on the fact that every Christian life also is a kind of theophany or rather "epiphany," namely a manifestation of God to the soul. This manifestation begins with the light of faith, given to us in baptism. In God's plan, this light is meant to increase steadily through life like the dawn of a beautiful day until it reaches the "full noon" of the beatific vision in heaven. Pray that this may be so in your life by your openness to the Word of God and the action of the Holy Eucharist. God **can** bring this about in you by the power of His Holy Spirit.

Selections

A. 40-55

40:1-11	The prologue: a herald of good news
40:12-29	The Creator and Redeemer
42:1-9	A light to the nations
52:13—53:12	The man of sorrows

B. 56-66

60:1-6	The glorious resurrection of Jerusalem
61:1-4	The mission of the prophet (see Lk. 4:16-22)
66:18-24	The new heavens and the new earth

C. 24-27, 34-35

25:6-10	The messianic banquet
35:1-10	They shall see the glory of God

Prayer: Psalm 48

"...in the city of our God."

Song: Zion, sing, break into song. Lucien Deiss (PMB-165)

Thought for the day: The grass withers, the flower fades, but the word of our God will stand forever (40:8).

JEREMIAH

The prophet
of the New Covenant

The call of the prophet took place around the year 626 B.C.—just a few decades before the final fall of Jerusalem (in 587 B.C.). The old world order in the Fertile Crescent, which for over two centuries had been held together by Assyrian might, was crumbling. In the ensuing international turmoil, the rising Babylonian nation was hoping to become the new master. It was during these critical years of Israel's history that Jeremiah had to perform his difficult prophetic task.

Ch 1   The call
    2:1—25:13b   Oracles against Judah and Jerusalem
    25:13c—25:38;
    and chs. 46-51   Oracles against the nations

N.B. Note how after 25 verses in chapter 25 (viz. 25:13c—25:38), this is interrupted until ch 46.

Chs 25-35 Prophecies of blessing
    36-45 Sufferings of Jeremiah
    46-51 Oracles against the nations
    52   Appendix. The fall of Jerusalem as Jeremiah had foretold. 586 B.C. (Extract from 2 K.14:18—25:30)

It fell to Jeremiah to interpret for his contemporaries the meaning of the coming fall of Jerusalem. From the first moment of his call, he felt the difficulty of his prophetic mission. Yet, during some forty years—often in the face of bitter persecution—he did not cease to tell the people the hard truth: God was about to permit the ruin of Jerusalem and the nation in order to lead them to repentance, forgiveness, and a return to God.

In the
New Testament

The great glory of Jeremiah is to have anticipated the teaching of the Gospel in many ways, in particular, the short oracle on the **new** Covenant (31:27-37). It has been called the prophet's spiritual testament to the world.

Read Lk. 22:20; 1 Co. 11:25; 2 Co. 3:6; Heb. 8:8-12.

In the present salvific moment

Jeremiah unflinchingly performed his appointed life's task without consideration for mere human respect and for what it cost him. Further, this prophet experienced within himself the suffering of his people, the suffering they had earned by their sins (cf. Jeremiah's confessions). Because of this the Fathers of the Church regard him as a prototype of Christ.

Points to think about

1. The book of Jeremiah, as it stands, is more like an anthology than a book. It makes difficult reading. You might use the following:

Prophetic Preaching			
	Chs 2-25	Chs 30-35	Chs 46-51
Mainly Narrative			
Ch 1 The Call	Chs 26-29	Chs 36-45	Ch 52

2. As you go through the book, highlight the passages that underscore the main themes of Jeremiah such as formalism in worship and interior religion, cf. 4:4, 8:8, etc.; the new Covenant, 31:31-34; God's purpose in human history.

Note particularly 31:31-34.

A new Covenant to replace the old one that was broken:

> v.31 The only time "new" Covenant is used in the Old Testament. (Ezekiel and Isaiah 2 would speak of an "everlasting" covenant.)

> v. 33 "I will write it upon their hearts." Interiorization of the Covenant (the Old Covenant was written on stone tablets (Ex. 31:18) or in a book (Ex. 24:7). See Jn. 4:19-24.

N.B. This Covenant is to be a completely "new" one ("not like the covenant I made with their fathers" v. 32).

> v. 34 In this new era ("Behold, the days are coming" v. 31), God Himself will intervene through His Holy Spirit (cf. Ezk. 36:26-27) and the forgiveness of sin: "They shall all know me"—the mystery of grace.

Thus the real newness announced here = (1) interiorization of the Covenant; (2) the new means used to assure faithfulness

3. Note in particular, Jeremiah's "confessions": passages that give us an insight into the interior life and struggles of Jeremiah: 11:18-23; 12:1-6; 15:10-21; 17:9-10, 14-18; 18:18-23; 20:7-12, 14-18.

4. Note also the parables and the symbolic actions used by the prophet to bring home his message, e.g., the potter (18:1f.).

5. Does Jeremiah's profoundly interior sense of communion with God illustrate what Martin Buber means by knowing God in the immediacy of "dialogue"?

6. Note how the greatness of Jeremiah's prophetic message is admirably seen in his attitude toward the great historical institutions of Israel, e.g., the temple (see 7:1-15), the law (8:8; 31:31-36), circumcision (4:4; 9:26; 6:10), the Davidic dynasty (22:30). Read these in the light of the "New Covenant" prophecy in 31:31-34.

7. Note short calendar of Jeremiah's life.

c 645   Born of a priestly family at Anatoth, a little village six miles from Jerusalem.

626   His call (Jeremiah is 19 years old.)

626-622 Years of apprenticeship. Call to conversion.

626-609 A new king: Josias. In the temple, the book of the Law is discovered (Deuteronomy). The Josian reform.

609   Calamity. Josias is killed in battle against the Pharaoh of Egypt.

605   Babylonian victory at Carchemish over Egypt.

597   First siege of Jerusalem. 1st deportation.

587-586 Second siege of Jerusalem. 2nd deportation. Jeremiah left behind. Later taken to Egypt where we lose sight of him.

Selections

Prophet's call. "Do not say, 'I am only a youth.'"

2:4-13   Israel's sin: they have abandoned me, the fountain of living water.

7:1-15   Formalism in worship: Do not say, "the temple of Jahweh, the temple, the temple."

20:7-18   A confession of Jeremiah: Why was I ever born?

31:27-37 The days to come: A new Covenant

Prayer: Jr. 20:7-13
"O Lord...who sees the heart and the mind."

Song: Hear, O Lord, the sound of my call. Ray Repp. (HYC I 20)

Thought for the day: "The course of man is not in his control, nor is it in man's power as he goes his way to guide his steps" (Jr. 10:23) (JB).

THE BOOK OF LAMENTATIONS

How could it ever
have happened!

The book of Lamentations is a series of five beautiful dirges inspired by the destruction of Jerusalem and the temple by the Babylonians in 587 B.C. In the English Bible, they are attributed to Jeremiah.

Ch 1 The desolation of Jerusalem
2 Why this has happened
3 God's purpose behind it: hope of mercy
4 The glorious past compared with the present misery
5 A prayer for the deliverance of Zion

This book describes in poignant and moving poetry the ruin of Jerusalem and the heart-rending misery of its desolate citizens. At the same time, it points out clearly that this calamity is a medicinal punishment from the hand of God, using Babylon as His instrument. In this way, the author tries to evoke sentiments of sorrow, amendment and conversion in his fellow countrymen: "The steadfast love of the Lord never ceases" (3:22).

In the
New Testament

The sentiments of Jeremiah and Ezekiel—so well expressed in these lamentations—have, as an undertone, the hope that this suffering has not been in vain. It is the lesson of the New Testament, too, that no human suffering need be in vain.
Read 2 Cor. 1:3-7.

In our life

The Church used these inspired verses of this book as an effective way of expressing her sorrow at the sufferings of Christ. We could also read them with the thought of persecuted Christians in mind, the so-called "Church of Silence."

Points to think about

1. The 5 poems differ slightly in literary form: 1 and 2 and 4 are more in the form of a dirge, while 3 is a personal lamentation, and 5 a collective lamentation and prayer.

2. There is a deep reason why the Septuagint and the Vulgate place them among the prophetical books. Although they are not prophecies in the strict sense of the word, they are imbued with the prophetical teaching and apply it to the crisis of 597-587 B.C., which was one of the greatest crises of faith in the history of the Chosen People.

Selections

1:1-7	The sad scene
2:13-19	The reason for it
3:22-23	Yet the Lord is still good
4:1-13	How could this ever have happened!

Prayer: Recite ch. 5 (with the thought of the "Church of Silence" in mind).

"Remember, O Lord, what has befallen us."

Song: There's a wideness in God's mercy. Ian D. Mitchell. (FEL - 6)

Thought for the day: The steadfast love of the Lord never ceases, his mercies never come to an end (3:22).

THE BOOK OF BARUCH
AND THE LETTER OF JEREMIAH

"Take courage, Jerusalem…" (4:30) (JB).

This book, although named after the famed secretary of Jeremiah, was, according to many scholars, possibly compiled by a Jew of the dispersion. It has been dated as late as the beginning of the second century B.C.

1:1-14	Introduction
1:15—3:8	Prayer of the exiles for forgiveness and restoration
3:9—4:4	True wisdom is found only in God's law, the law given to Israel.
4:5—5:9	A prayerful poem: hope for the future
6:1-72	The letter of Jeremiah to the exiles in Babylon: lifeless idols and the living God.

In this book, the author, posing as the famous secretary of Jeremiah, instructs and encourages his readers. Because of its possible late date, it has been considered a retrospective view of earlier times. In many aspects, its language is close to that of the Wisdom movement which flourished after the return from exile. Apparently it was much in use during these last centuries of the Old Testament period.

In the
New Testament

The future messianic glory of Jerusalem pictured in this book and its splendid monotheism are like rays of the morning sun announcing New Testament times, now close at hand.

Read Mt. 13:10-17.

In our life

As we read this book, we could ask ourselves whether we sufficiently realize our good fortune in living in these messianic times of the New Testament, times which so many righteous men of the Old Testament longed to see.

Points to think about

1. The letter of Jeremiah which is chapter 6 of the book of Baruch is actually considered by scholars to have been written sometime during the Greek period. It is a powerful warning against idolatry.

2. Compare this book with Isaiah chs. 40-66.

Selections

    1:1—3:8 Temple worship in Jerusalem
    3:9—4:4 True wisdom is found only in God's law.
    4:5—5:9 Prayer for the happy return of the exiles and for the future messianic glory of Jerusalem.

Prayer: Recite 3:1-8 for the "Church of Silence."

Song: Get up Jerusalem. C. P. Mudd. (WLSM)

Thought for the day: "See the joy that is coming to you from God" (Ba. 4:36b) (JB).

EZEKIEL

A new hope

"A new heart I will give you, and a new spirit I will put within you" (36:26).

Ezekiel was one of the exiles who, along with King Jehoiakin and prominent citizens of Judah, was taken to Babylonia in 597 B.C., in that first wave of deportations. With his fellow citizens, he settled by the banks of the river Chebar, a short distance from Babylon. There, as narrated in the opening lines of the book, he was seized "by the hand of God."

1-4   Ezekiel's call and mission
5-24   Oracles against Judah and Jerusalem: the worst is yet to come (possibly before 587 B.C.)
25-32 Oracles against Judah's neighboring nations (These are not in chronological order.)
33-39 In and after 587 B.C., Ezekiel gives back hope: oracles of the restoration of Israel
40-48 Vision of the New Jerusalem

Ezekiel's entire teaching seems to center on one basic topic: inner conversion. This was necessary if Israel was to make a fresh beginning and be received into the eternal covenant of peace God was going to make with them. Israel had to achieve a "new heart" and a "new spirit" (18:31) or rather God Himself would bestow a "new heart" and "infuse his own spirit" in them. In this way they will really be "God's People" (36:26). Thus will be inaugurated God's eternal covenant of peace with them (37:26).

In the New Testament

Ezekiel, in line with his great predecessors, Isaiah and Jeremiah, underlines the importance of the effusion of the Spirit. This was to characterize the messianic age. We see this fulfilled in the New Testament in the Gospel and the life of the early Church.

Read Acts 2:1-21.

In the present salvific moment

Ezekiel takes great pains to emphasize the importance of individual responsibility (see ch. 18:1-32). An authentic spiritual life can only be based on a sense of personal responsibility before God, the kind of life that makes one a true member of the Church, the New Jerusalem, "which is being built as a city whose foundation is Christ."

Points to think about

1. Underline the passages and lines which underscore the basic ideas of Ezekiel's message: e.g., the holiness of God (cf. 1:1—3:27); departure of Jahweh's glory (10:1-22) and the return of God back to Jerusalem (43:1-12); individual responsibility (18:1-32); Good Shepherd (ch. 34); a new heart and a new spirit (36:26); etc.

2. Read carefully the lines and passages that speak of the giving of the Spirit, e.g., ch. 36:26, 37:1-14; Is. 11:1-3, 32:15-19, 42:1, 44:3, 61:1; Jr. 31:31f., later Jl. 3:1-2. And later in the New Testament, see Mt. 3:13-17; Lk. 1:35, 41, 67, etc.; Jn. 1:32f., 3:6, 4:24, 14:25; Rm. 8:11; 1 Co. 6:11, etc.

3. Compare and contrast the description of the call of the prophet in Ezekiel (1:1—3:21) with the call of Isaiah (ch. 6) and that of Jeremiah (ch. 1) to see the descriptive style of Ezekiel.

4. One of the impressive passages of Ezekiel is the withdrawal of God from Jerusalem because of its sins (10:1-22). We live in a society which is secularized to such an extent that God seems to enter less and less into the deliberations of statesmen. Can we do something about this?

5. How does Ezekiel's teaching on individual responsibility (cf. 14:12-23, ch. 18, 33:10-20) mark a decisive advance in the development of moral teaching in the Old Testament (cf. Gn. 6:18, 18:22-23; Dt. 5:9; Jr. 31:29)?

6. What purpose did the exile of the Chosen People serve in God's plan of salvation for all mankind?

Selections

1:1-28	The call of the prophet
10:1-22	Departure of Jahweh's glory from Jerusalem
18:1-32	Individual responsibility: a new heart
24:15-27	Death of Ezekiel's wife and the news of Jerusalem's fall
34:11-31	The Good Shepherd and the covenant of peace
36:24-28	The giving of the Spirit: internal renewal
37:1-14	Vision of the valley of dry bones (Nothing is impossible to God.)
43:1-12	The return of the glory of Jahweh back to Jerusalem
48:30-35	The city of Jerusalem

Prayer: Psalm 137:1-6.
By the streams of Babylon, there we sat and wept....

Song: By the streams of Babylon. Ps. 137. Gelineau. or/and Be consoled, my People. Parker. (WLSM)

Thought for the day: I will put my spirit within you and you shall live (37:14).

DANIEL

The meaning
of history

We are in about the year 165 B.C. The country is occupied by the Seleucids of Syria. The ruling king was Antiochus IV (175-163 B.C.), called "Epiphanes" because he claimed to be "god-manifest." A fanatic apostle of Hellenism, he had proscribed the Jewish religion, forbade its practice, profaned the temple and even turned it into a seat of the worship of Zeus. Persecution was aflame. Shortly after the outbreak of the Maccabean wars, occasioned by this persecution, an unknown writer composed the book of Daniel—a cryptic message of encouragement and hope for the persecuted.

Chs. 1-6   Stories about Daniel and his companions
     7-12   Daniel's visions.
  13-14 Two anecdotes: 1. Susanna
                       2. Daniel against the idols

Writing at a time when the institution of prophecy had almost ceased in Israel, the author adapted the message of the prophets to the situation of his own time. Utilizing the literary form that has come to be known as the apocalyptic, he interpreted for the people the meaning of the happenings they were going through. In other words, he was writing a kind of theology of history, an explanation of historical events in the light of faith.

In the
New Testament

In the two centuries preceding the Christian era, many currents of thought were moving through Judaism—currents that would naturally influence the early Christian community and the New Testament writers. The book of Revelation is written in an idiom that is very similar to the book of Daniel and possibly had a similar purpose and message. Like the book of Daniel, it too was probably intended to inspire and encourage the suffering, persecuted Christians of the end of the first century of our era. Here too the author explains the significance of the human drama in the light of his faith.

Read the book of Revelation 12:7-17, 20:1—21:6

In the present salvific moment

Today men seem to be living out their lives in the shadow of a nuclear cloud, and modern man is becoming increasingly skeptical about whether or not there is meaning in history. Consequently, the book of Daniel makes very relevant reading. For its message is that in spite of appearances to the contrary, history is not controlled by the recklessness of men or by blind fate. For reasons known only to Him, God may permit many things. But the final issues are in the hands of God, rather than in human hands. With such a conviction born of faith, we can live and act with hope. The whole of history is like a drama which, from beginning to end, is directed in a mysterious way according to the sovereign plan of God.

Points to think about

1. Daniel is the name of a traditional, pious Israelite. In the Bible, in the late post-exilic period, it was customary to release writings under the name of some figure of ancient Jewish tradition.

2. The book of Daniel should be read with the general background of the books of the Maccabees in mind, since it is basically a message of encouragement to the persecuted people of God. In part one, chapters 1-6, the six anecdotes from the life and times of Daniel show examples of perseverance in the faith in the midst of difficulties and bring home the lesson that God is the Lord of history.

1. The trial of Daniel and his friends (ch. 1)
2. Nebuchadnezzar's dream (ch. 2)
   Human wisdom is nothing compared to the wisdom given by God.
3. The three confessors in the fiery furnace (idolatry) (ch. 3)
   God saves His faithful ones.
4. Nebuchadnezzar's madness (ch. 4)
   No human greatness can take pride before God.
5. Belshazzar's feast (ch. 5)
   God is the master of history.
6. Daniel in the lion's den (ch. 6)
   God protects His faithful ones.

3. Looking backward from the time of the Maccabees, four successive kingdoms are pictured in chs. 2, 7, and 8 —the Babylonian, the Median, the Persian and the Greek. The accumulation of oppression is finally concentrated in one kingdom (the Seleucid) and in one persecutor king, Antiochus Epiphanes.

Part 2: A dream and three visions

1. The vision of the four beasts (7:1-28)
2. The vision of the ram and the he-goat (8:1-27)
   The taller horn symbolizes the Persians triumphing over the Medes. The he-goat = Greek empire.
3. The dream and prophecy of the 70 weeks (9:1-27)
   See Jr. 25:11-12, 29:10, on the exile and the return: a reflection.
4. The vision of the last days (10:1—12:13)
   The age of the Seleucids and the Ptolemies, up to Antiochus Epiphanes, in greater detail

4. One of the contributions of the book of Daniel to the development of revelation in the Old Testament is the doctrine of the future life. But unlike the book of Wisdom, which was in some way influenced by the Greek notion of immortality, in the book of Daniel it is presented in the light of Hebrew thought. The resurrection

of the body is portrayed as occurring at the end of time, when God's victory over the powers of evil will be complete (see 12:1-4).

5. The word "apocalyptic" comes from the Greek word "apokalyptein" meaning "to uncover or reveal." With the book of Daniel, we enter fully into this type of literature called the apocalyptic, a type that was born of prophetism. The theme and the message, presented with a great variety of pictures and symbols, is similar to that of the prophets, and although looking to the future, it is primarily concerned with the meaning of the present and the past, the meaning of history. It has been called prophecy in a new idiom.

The apocalyptic writers put the accent on the final great act of God's intervention in history—that unique divine initiative at the end of history when God will not allow human freedom to interfere any more with His purposes. God created the world. He created it for a purpose and He will achieve this purpose, in His own time, with or without human cooperation, or rather, in spite of the perversity of the human will. This optimism born of faith in God—that God is present in history, not as a mere helpless spectator, but rather that He is in control of things, (in spite of contrary appearances)—was already there in the prophets. Hence the apocalyptic literature has been considered a true child of prophecy.

This hope is presented with a sense of urgency as an encouragement to the just who are going through a difficult time. Yet, a little while and the day of suffering will be over and the great Day to which all history has been moving will dawn.

Apocalyptic literature saw its heyday about the Maccabean age, from about 200 B.C. to about 200 A.D.

During this time, besides the inspired books of Daniel in the Old Testament and the book of Revelation in the New Testament, many other books appeared such as the book of Enoch (dividing world history into 7 periods and then the finale), the book of Jubilees, the testament of the 12 patriarchs (i.e., the last words of the sons of

Jacob), some of the Qumran literature; then later in the 1st century A.D. came works like the Assumption of Moses, the life of Adam and Eve, the Ascension of Isaiah, the apocalypse of Abraham, etc. The 2nd century A.D. produced works like the apocalypses of Peter, the apocryphal infancy gospels, the Acts of John, Peter, etc.

Selections

Ch. 12 The goal of history is God's kingdom—not any human kingdom or utopia of human planning.

7 The vision of the four beasts arising out of the sea

6 Daniel in the lion's den. God is able to deliver His faithful ones.

9 The 72 weeks—kingdom of God near at hand

Prayer: Recite Daniel 2:20-23.

He changes times and seasons.

O Lord, we pray for the leaders of the nations of the world. Guide them by Your almighty power in the momentous decisions they must make for the safety and welfare of all mankind. Through Christ our Lord. Amen.

Song: O God, our help in ages past. Isaac Watts. (FEL - 53)

Thought for the day: "May the name of God be blessed forever and ever.... His, to control the procession of times and seasons, to make and unmake kings" (Dn. 2:20, 21) (JB).

HOSEA

The prophet
of God's love

"I will betroth you to me forever" (2:19).

Hosea was the successor of Amos in the prophetic office in the Northern Kingdom. Thus, historically, the book of Hosea comes after Amos, although in the Bible, it is placed before. His prophetic career apparently extended from the last part of the long reign of Jeroboam II (784-744 B.C.) through some of the years of political instability and confusion that followed. The country was in a state of confusion, demoralization and anxiety (4 kings were assassinated within a period of 15 years). The terrible Assyrian advance on Palestine struck terror into the hearts of all. Just as God's word through Amos was about justice and punishment at a time when all seemed well, so now when things were really bad, His word through Hosea was about love and mercy.

Chs. 1-3   The marriage of Hosea : a symbol!
4:1—14:1   Israel's sins and the punishment they merit
14:2-10   Conversion and future happiness

The deep note struck in the book of Hosea is that God's judgments are redemptive. Even in punishment, God's purpose is not to destroy but to save. God's love is greater and deeper than man's infidelity. In trying to bring this home to the people, Hosea uses not only the image of father and child as in the book of Exodus and Deuteronomy, but also that of husband and wife.

In the
New Testament

Hosea provides a salutary corrective to the idea that the God of the Old Testament is only a God of justice and punishment. In this book, we see the beginnings of the doctrine of the New Testament that God is love. The message of Hosea gains a new dimension of depth because of the cross of Christ.

Read 1 Jn. 4:7-18.

Points to think about

1. Highlight the following and try to see their significance for the general theme of the book of Hosea: 1:9; 2:1, 16, 21; 4:2, 6; 5:1; 6:6; 8:1; 11:1, 3, 4, 9; 12:6.

2. Compare and contrast the picture of God presented in Hosea with that of Amos.

3. Hosea was the first Israelite prophet to interpret the Covenant by comparing it with marriage. This image is taken up by the prophetic tradition. See, for example, Jr. 2:1-2, 20-21; 3:1-5; Ezk. chs. 16 and 23; Is. 50:1-3; 54:4-6; 61:10-11; 62:4-5, etc. (Jr. 3:19-20 juxtaposes the two images of father and child, husband and wife.) It is also taken up into the New Testament and is found in the Gospels (e.g., Mt. 22:1-4, 25:1-13), in the epistles (e.g., Ep. 5:25-33) and in the last pages of the Bible: "I saw the holy city, the new Jerusalem, coming down from God out of heaven, as beautiful as a bride all dressed for her husband" (Rv. 21:2).

4. Regarding the story of the conjugal life of Hosea in chs. 1 and 3, there are two questions discussed by scholars. One regards the historicity of the event. The other concerns the order of events. Regarding the former, many scholars today are inclined to consider the story as real rather than just allegorical; compare Jeremiah's celibacy (16:1), Ezekiel's loss of his wife (24:18), Isaiah and his children (8:18).

Regarding the order of events in chs. 1 and 3, some think that we have two episodes from the life of Hosea and others that these chapters are two parallel accounts of the same event (with additional details in ch. 3).

5. In view of Hosea's message, what should be our practical attitude toward God in daily life?

Selections

1:2-9   Hosea's marriage: his three children
2:16-21   The Lord's love for His people
6:1-6   What I want is love, not sacrifice.
11:1-9   God's love is deeper than man's infidelity.

Prayer: Recite Psalm 103.
He does not deal with us according to our sins.

Song: Amazing grace. Negro spiritual.

Thought for the day: "Hold fast to love and justice and wait continually for your God" (12:6).

JOEL

The outpouring of the Spirit

"I will pour out my spirit..." (3:1) (JB).

It is difficult to date the work of Joel. He is, however, generally assigned some time in the period between 500 and 350 B.C., possibly around 400 B.C. On the occasion of a locust plague of unusual severity, Joel draws a picture of divine judgment on the final day of the Lord.

1.	1:1—2:27	Concern for the present: the locust plague
A. (a)	1:2-12	The ruin of the country
(b)	1:13-20	Call to repentance and prayer
(c)	2:1-11	A second description of the plague
(d)	2:12-17	A second call to repentance and prayer
B.	2:18-27	Prayer answered
2.	3:1—4:21	Apocalyptic hope for the future: the Day of Jahweh and the New Age
	3:1-5	The outpouring of the Spirit
	4:1-17	The judgment of the nations
	4:18-21	The glorious future of Israel

Joel's combination of a concern for the present with an apocalyptic hope for the future was not something entirely new in prophetic literature. But his most significant contribution is the promise of the outpouring of God's Spirit in messianic times on **all** believers without exception, men, women, children, even slaves (3:1-5). In the New Age God would reveal Himself, not only as He always does, in His powerful, moral control of nature and history, but also through His Spirit from within (cf. Jn. 4:21-24).

In the
New Testament

Joel opens out perspectives, which his contemporaries did not and perhaps, could not, at the moment, fully understand. But when, in the "fullness of time," from the day of Pentecost onwards, the Holy Spirit began to be given to the primitive Church (the New People of Israel), to all, old and young, rich and poor, even slaves, the real significance of this extraordinary text of Joel became clear.

Read Ac. 2:14-21.

In the present salvific moment

"All who call on the name of the Lord will be saved" (Jl. 3:5). This salvation through faith is extended by Peter in his Pentecostal sermon (cited above) and by Paul in his epistles (cf. Rm. 10:13) to include all nations and peoples regardless of race, time and place. The divine election calls for man's response in faith (Jl. 3:5, Ga. 3:27-29).

Points to think about

1. As you go through the text, highlight lines that bring out the different aspects of Joel's message: e.g., the importance of worship (1:9, 13, 15; 2:13), universalism (3:1, 2), salvation through the response of faith (3:5), need of repentance (2:12-17), the giving of the Spirit (3:1-5). Note the difference in the numbering of the chapters in different Bibles. The numbering followed in this chapter is that of the Jerusalem Bible.

2. Like other post-exilic prophets (e.g., Haggai, Zechariah), Joel regards the regular performance of worship as extremely important, but, with Malachi, Ezekiel, Jeremiah and others, he perceives that the essence of true religion is in the inner attitude (Joel 2:13) rather than in outward rites.

3. The description of the invasion of the locusts in chs. 1-2 has been variously interpreted: a) literally, i.e., an actual locust plague at the time; (b) allegorically, that is, invasions in the past; (c) apocalyptically, i.e., supernatural creatures at the end of time; (d) a combination of one or more views. In general, however, most authors would agree that there seems to be here a real invasion of swarms of locusts.[1]

4. There is no time or date indicated in the text. This fact has left the question of the date an open one. But the marked post-exilic characteristics of the book (e.g., its partial particularism, emphasis on cult, etc.) and its apparent dependence on exilic and post-exilic prophets such as Ezekiel, Zechariah, and Malachi help to date Joel as post-exilic.

5. The clear division of the text into main divisions or sections (see above) has raised the question of the unity of the book. But in the light of the unity of style, content, message and uniform historical background, the question ceases to be pertinent.

6. In a certain sense, Pentecost is not the feast of a day, nor even of a ·season. It is an aspect of Christian life. In this sense, Pentecost continues right now in the Church and in the world. Pray that God's Holy Spirit may continue to work in the world through the hearts of all who believe.

Selections

    2:1-11   The plague of locusts
    2:12-17 Call to repentance and prayer
    3:1-5   The outpouring of the Spirit
    4:15-21 The Day of Jahweh and the future glory of
               Jerusalem

---

1. On this, see Aage Bentzen, **Introduction to the Old Testament,** II (Copenhagen: G.E.C. Gad, 1967), p. 134.

Prayer: Psalm 104.

When you send forth your Spirit, they are created and you renew the face of the earth.

Song: Grant to us, O Lord, a heart renewed. Lucien Deiss. (PMB-165).

Thought for the day: "Let your hearts be broken, not your garments torn" (2:13) (JB).

AMOS

The "prophet of God's justice"

"Let justice roll down like waters..." (5:24).

Many years had elapsed since the reigns of David and Solomon. A new enemy had arisen to threaten the now-divided kingdom. The people of the wealthy, northern kingdom (Israel or Samaria) grew more and more idolatrous as the years passed, straying ever further from fidelity to the Covenant. God spoke to them through Amos, the prophet.

1:1	Title
1:2	Introduction
1:3—2:16	Judgment on Israel and her neighbors
3:1—6:14	Special warning to the People of God
7:1—9:10	Five visions
9:11-15	Words of hope: restoration and Messianic prosperity

Amos was called from trimming sycamore trees to the great task of a prophet of God. In plain but forceful language, he points out the sins of God's People. His denunciations are aimed, in particular, at the callous-hearted rich and their false piety, which would certainly bring down God's chastisement.

In the New Testament

In the New Testament, in a way reminiscent of the prophet Amos, the apostle James reprimands rich people who care nothing about the norms of social justice.
Read James 5:1-6.

"Your riches have rotted and your garments are moth eaten."

In our life

The liturgical prayer of the Church often reminds us of the necessary link between our religious life and the social mission of the Church. We must live in the consciousness that we are God's children and that all men are our brothers. Otherwise, our worship becomes pure formalism, and then hypocritical.

Points to think about

1. Many of the Israelites had come to feel that just because they were the Chosen People, God had to make good His promises to them regardless of their conduct. The prophets gave a different meaning to the idea of being "chosen." Later St. Paul, writing to Christians, would reflect: If God did not spare the natural branches, neither will he spare you (Rm. 11:21).

2. The political background of Amos' prophecy is worth noting. He prophesied during the long reign of Jeroboam II (784-744). Egypt was in eclipse (politically). Assyria was not yet on the war path with Tiglath-Pileser III. There was tranquility, peace and prosperity. But, beneath these trappings of prosperity, Amos discerns a profound moral disorder mainly due to social injustice, corrupt practices in everyday business life, exploitation and the misery of the poor. Nor was all well with the cult in the sanctuaries, especially at Bethel, the royal sanctuary, due to idolatry, temple prostitution, etc.

3. Although a shepherd of Tekoa (6 miles south of Jerusalem), who tended sycamore trees in the springtime, Amos was not completely uneducated, as his style shows. Note the short, forceful sentences, neat phrases and word plays.

4. Note the main points of his message:
   1. He calls his contemporaries to a more profound understanding of the Covenant and a life led according to that Covenant.

2. In default of this, the "day of Jahweh" will come through the Assyrians.

3. Only a complete change of heart can save the nation.

4. Whatever may happen, a remnant of just men will survive, Israel will rise again, and God's plans will be realized through a descendant of David.

5. Amos has been called the "Karl Marx" of the Old Testament. But was Amos a revolutionary in the modern sense of the term? Did he advocate revolution by downtrodden masses or did he limit himself to his God-given task of reminding the people of their moral obligations and of the fact that God is there to judge?

N.B. On the feast of Christ, the King, the Church prays that God's kingdom may come in our midst, "a kingdom of truth and life, a kingdom of holiness and grace, a kingdom of justice, love and peace." Resolve to do your part in making this prayer a reality.

Selections

Ch. 1   The theme of the prophet's preaching
4:1-12   The sins of Israel
6:1-8   Indictment of the callous rich
9:11-15 A ray of hope: the remnant theme

Prayer: Psalm 82
"Give justice to the weak and the fatherless."

Song: So said Amos the prophet. Casey. C.S.S.R. (YC)

Thought for the day: I will give heed to the way that is blameless (Ps. 101).

OBADIAH

The guilt
of Edom

"As you have done, it shall be done to you" (v. 15).

The book of Obadiah, the shortest in the Bible, is an oracle against Edom, Judah's neighbor. It foretells the destruction of Edom because of its consistently unfraternal attitude toward Judah. There is no certain evidence as to the date of its composition except that it looks back to the fall of Jerusalem (587 B.C.) and forward to the destruction of Edom, which took place sometime in the 5th or 4th century B.C.

Vs. 1-18 The "Day of Jahweh" for Edom
19-21 A new Israel

Despite the fact that the two countries were traditionally related according to the story of the twin brothers, Jacob and Esau (cf. Gn. 25:23), the Edomites refused passage through their country to the Israelites on their way to the promised land (Nb. 20:18). This hostility continued through the period of the monarchy. More than one prophet inveighed against them (cf. Am. 1:11-12; Jr. 49:7-22; Ezk. 25:12-14; Ps. 137:7). They not only rejoiced over the destruction of Jerusalem but seized part of the territory of Judah afterwards (cf. Ml. 1:2-5). The prophet tells them that the Day of the Lord is coming upon them too.

In the
New Testament

This hostility between the two brother nations reflects the painfulness of the relationship of man to man (cf. Gn. 1-11). One takes delight in another's distress, one profits by another's misfortunes, one stands aside to let another suffer. Obadiah suggests an application, on the national scale, of certain parables of Jesus.

Read Lk. 10:25-37.
Who is my neighbor?

161

In the present salvific moment

The prophets, here as elsewhere, point beyond all our conflicts, all our suspicions, all our wars, to the Kingdom where God reigns and will reign by the power of His grace. "The kingdom shall be the Lord's."

Points to think about

1. Does Obadiah resemble the prophecy of Nahum? In what sense?

2. Is it correct to isolate the book of Obadiah from the rest of the prophetic thought?

3. Even taken by itself, can we see this cry of vengeance as a point in a long journey (taking the Bible as a whole) that would lead even to love of enemies in the New Testament?

4. As shown in the book of Genesis (chs. 1-11), sin is the real cause of alienation and separation among the nations. But God has renewed all creation in Christ. Subjection to His rule will reunite all nations in a lasting peace (See the liturgy of the feast of Christ the King).

Selections

v. 2-4   Sentence on Edom
v. 10-15 The guilt of Edom
v. 19-21 The new Israel

Prayer: Psalm 133
"How good, how delightful it is for all to live together like brothers" (JB).

Song: If you bring your gift to the altar. Lucien Deiss. (BHP-II 88)

Thought for the day: You should not have gloated over your brother in the day of his misfortune (v. 12).

JONAH

Beyond frontiers
of race and religion

"...that my salvation may reach to the end of the earth" (Is. 49:6).

The circumstances of the time after the return from exile called for the great reforms enacted by Ezra and Nehemiah. The Jewish people were in danger of absorption and gradual disappearance by syncretism in religion and inter-marriage with non-Jewish peoples. Nevertheless, as in most reforms, there was the tendency to go to the other extreme, to a narrow exclusivism in race and religion, considering the latter as the necessary condition of God's favor. Possibly at this period there appeared this little book with a lofty message, a message presented in the guise of a story.

1:1-16	Jonah flees from the mission given him by God.
2:1-10	A psalm of thanksgiving
2:11—3:10	The unwilling missionary
4:1-11	The senselessness of limiting God's mercy

The story is a lesson to the Jewish people that other peoples and other nations, even the most cruel enemies of Israel, were not beyond the pale of God's mercy. The ludicrous picture that the author draws of Jonah's behavior was an implicit rebuke to his Jewish contemporaries that God's purpose in history was not restricted to the preservation of the Jewish community. It was a vigorous reminder in the spirit of "second" Isaiah that Israel's call and mission carried with it a great responsibility: to be a light to the nations so that God's salvation may reach to the ends of the earth (Is. 49:6, Gn. 12:3).

163

In the
New Testament

The words of John the Baptist, "Do not presume to say to yourselves, we have Abraham for our father, for I tell you, God is able from these stones to raise up children to Abraham" (Mt. 3:9), and those of Christ: "Many shall come from the east and from the west and shall sit down in the kingdom of heaven" (Lk. 13:29) emphasize in no uncertain terms the universality of God's call to salvation.

In the present salvific moment

The declaration of the Second Vatican Council on "Non-Christian religions" is a reminder to us of the message of the book of Jonah: that no one is outside God's providence and that Christians are not the only ones comprehended by God's redemptive action (cf. 1 Tm. 2:5 and Ga. 3:28). This declaration is a call to all Christians to do their part in bringing about the realization of the world-wide mission of the Church, the new people of Israel.

Points to think about

1. Considerations of vocabulary, background and theme have led scholars to the conclusion that the book was written in the period after the exile, presumably sometime around the fourth century B.C., although a prophet by the name of Jonah is mentioned in 2 Kings (14:25).

2. It is generally agreed among scholars today that this is not necessarily a biographical account of an actual experience lived through by the prophet Jonah but could be a short story or parable written to bring home to its readers a message.

3. Highlight the lines that bring out God's gracious goodness and mercy, on the one hand, and the petty exclusiveness of Jonah shown in his words and behavior, on the other.

4. The book of Jonah, like the rest of the books of the Bible, should be read in the context of the whole Bible

and God's universal plan of salvation contained already in the call and promise to Abraham (cf. Gn. 12:3, 22:18).

5. The present world torn asunder by prejudice and antagonisms (racial, national, ideological) makes a ludicrous picture like that of Jonah in the background of the great goodness and love of God for all men: God would redeem, man would destroy without mercy.

6. "So much for my will. Show me what is Yours," wrote Abraham Lincoln in his struggle to know the will of God. That was in pleasant contrast to Jonah, who ran from the will of God. Where do we stand?

7. The Bible often shows us, as in the case of Nineveh, that God "changes His mind" as man changes his conduct. In this sense, it could be said that God has placed our destiny in our own hands.

8. The Church in her liturgy envisions a day when from the rising of the sun even to its setting, God's name may be praised among all nations. (See the Mass for Mission Sunday.) May this vision become ours too.

Selections

    1:1-16 The uselessness of trying to escape from God's presence without or within
    4:1-11 The great goodness of God and the petty selfishness of man

Prayer: Psalm 67

"Let the nations be glad and sing for joy."

(A remarkable thing about this psalm is that God's blessing on Israel is taken to be a sign of His salvation for all nations.)

Song: All you peoples, clap your hands. Ray Repp. (HYC 14)

Thought for the day: I knew that you are a God of tenderness and compassion, slow to anger, rich in graciousness, relenting from evil (4:2) (cf. JB).

MICAH

The sower
of unrest and hope

"Jerusalem shall become a heap of ruins" (3:12).

Micah was a contemporary of Isaiah in the southern kingdom. According to Mi. 1:1, the prophet functioned during the reigns of Jotham, Achaz and Hezekiah, a period of nearly 50 years (740 B.C.—687 B.C.). During this time, Samaria was captured by Sargon II of Assyria (721 B.C.) and Jerusalem besieged by the Assyrian, Sennacherib (701 B.C.).

Ch. 1—3	Oracles of woe: threats of punishment
4—5	Promises of future blessings
6:1—7:7	Oracles of woe: denunciations and threats
7:8-20	Promise of future restoration

Micah was to the southern kingdom of Judah what Amos had been to the northern kingdom of Israel. Convinced of the justice and holiness of God, Micah announces the consequences of the sins of the people and preaches repentance and conversion (cf. Mi. 2-3, 6:9-11). At the same time, penetrated with the idea of the divine goodness and mercy, he sustains and encourages when misfortune strikes.

In the
New Testament

The prophet Micah in 5:1-2 looks back to the very origins of King David (from Bethlehem) as the source from which the One awaited would come. Although Micah's text does not make its appearance in rabbinic literature about the Messiah until quite late, the popular belief in the 1st century B.C. that the Messiah would be born in Bethlehem is reflected in both Matthew and John.

Read Mt. 2:1-8; Jn. 7:40-44.

In our life

Micah draws our attention to the great qualities that count in life in his beautiful words:

"He has showed you, O man, what is good;
and what does the Lord require of you
but to do justice, and to love kindness,
and to walk humbly with your God" (6:8).

Points to think about

1. What lesson or lessons can we draw from Micah 3:10f. (such as that man is more important than his work)?

2. Are all equally responsible for national calamities permitted by God—what would Micah say today? (cf. 3:1-12)

3. Highlight the significant verse (6:8) where he, as it were, summarizes the messages of his predecessors, Amos, Hosea and Isaiah.

Selections

1:10-16 The alarm
2:1-10   Jerusalem's men of wealth
5:1-8   Appeal to the leaders: a glorious future

Prayer: Pray Micah 7:14-20.
"...delighting in showing mercy" (JB).

Song: Have mercy, Lord. Quinlan (YCH)

Thought for the day: To do justice and to love kindness and to walk humbly with your God (6:8).

NAHUM

"A pool whose waters run away" (2:8)

During a whole century, Assyria had inspired terror in the hearts of the people of the whole of the Fertile Crescent, its capital city soaked in blood, "full of lies and booty" (3:1). Toward the end of the 8th century B.C., the power of this mighty nation began to wane. Nahum sees in the fall and destruction of Nineveh (612 B.C.), God's punishment of Assyria for misusing the great power given to her.

Ch. 1   The action of God's judgment in the world

2 & 3 The end of Nineveh

The message that God, and not man, is, in the ultimate analysis, the maker of history comes again and again in the prophetic preaching. "The Lord is slow to anger and of great might" (1:3).

In the New Testament

The prophecy of Nahum gives a vivid picture of the intense feelings of nationalism and joy that the fall of Nineveh occasioned in Judean hearts. To avoid a misunderstanding of the prophet's apparently one-sided oracle, it should be balanced off by the lesson of universal salvation presented in Jonah and the love of enemies taught in the New Testament.

Read Mt. 5:38-48.

In our lives

The message presented with the unvarnished, forceful language of Nahum depicting the sack of Nineveh is a strong reminder of the inevitable fate that awaits all tyrants: "All who draw the sword will die by the sword" (Mt. 26:52). And those who suffer under intolerable regimes in totalitarian countries can take courage from the words of Nahum, "God is slow to anger and of great might" (1:3).

Points to think about

1. Highlight the lines or sections giving the religious message of Nahum that God is Lord of history, e.g., 1:3.

2. Note the vivid and forceful phrases that make Nahum sound almost like an eyewitness account of the battle, e.g., 3:3.

3. Unlike other prophets, this short prophecy has only one subject: Nineveh and the sentence of God's justice on its wickedness. This explains why it could give the impression of a certain spiritual weakness, as a giving in to feelings of vengeance. It is, actually, more like a cry of relief than a full-fledged prophecy. "Keep your feasts, O Judah, fulfill your vows, for never again shall the wicked come against you; he is utterly cut off" (2:1).

Selections

    1:1-8   The Lord of history
    2:2-10 The assault
    3:1-11 The end

Prayer: Psalm 82
    "Rise, O God; judge the earth, for yours are all the nations" (NAB).

Song: Well, it's a new day. Mifflern. (WLSM)

Thought for the day: "The Lord is slow to anger and of great might" (1:3).

HABAKKUK

A prophet's problem

"I will stand on my watchtower...watching to see... what answer he will make to my complaints" (Hab. 2:1) (JB).

The most probable historical background of the book lies in the period of the beginning of the Babylonian invasions (about 600 B.C.). It was, by now, evident that Judah would be punished by this new imperial power which was as bad, if not worse than Assyria: "marching miles across the country to seize the homes of others... scooping up prisoners like sand" (cf. 1:6,9) (JB).

1:1—2:4	The dialogue between the prophet and God (2 complaints of the prophet, each of which is followed by an answer from God)
2:5—2:20	Curse on the oppressor (5 curses describing the manner of acting of the Babylonians)
ch. 3	Plea to God for His intervention

The prophet's problem is the problem of evil. He wondered how God's justice could be served by a sinful nation like Judah being punished by a still more sinful and lawless nation like Babylon. To this perplexing problem, the prophet finds no immediate answer except to take his stand on this "watchtower of faith" (2:1-4).

In the New Testament

Habakkuk was one of the first in the Old Testament frankly to pose the problem of evil. This question would gradually be seen in greater depth in later years in Israel (cf. Wisdom books like Job). But the real existential answer to this existential problem would be fully illustrated only in the New Testament when God turned the worst that man could do to a good end.

Read Ph. 3:7-14: "That I may know him and the power of his resurrection."

In our life

A Christian faced with the inexplicable trouble and difficulties of life can lift up his eyes to the Lord with the prophet when he received the answer to his prayer. "Behold he whose soul is not upright in him shall fail, but the righteous shall live by his faithfulness" (2:4).

Points to think about

1. Highlight the lines and phrases that bring out the prophet's problem and the answer to it, e.g., 1:1-4, 12-13; 2:1-4.

2. Highlight the phrases describing the advance of Babylon and its lawlessness. See for example, 1:6-11.

3. Note the beauty of the poem in chapter 3, especially the expression of unconquerable trust in the closing lines (vv. 17-19).

4. Is the prophet's problem adequately answered in the book? If not, what is the answer? Do you find it in the Bible?

Selections

1:5-11	The terrible invader
1:12-17	The prophet's problem
2:1-4	The answer
3:1-6, 19	The prophet's prayer

Prayer: Recite 3:2, 3, 10-19.
"God, the Lord, is my strength."

Song: The Lord is my shepherd. Ray Repp. (F.E.L. - 132)

Thought for the day: "The righteous shall live by his faithfulness" (2:4).

ZEPHANIAH

The day
is near

"The great day of the Lord is near, near and hastening fast" (1:14).

For some fifty or sixty years Micah and Isaiah had ceased to speak. The northern kingdom was no more. The Assyrian invasion of 701 B.C. had left the little kingdom of Judah in a state of devastation and subject to the invader. Sometime around 625 B.C. in the reign of King Josias, Zephaniah proclaimed with a sense of urgency: the great day of Jahweh is near, near and coming with all speed.

1:2—2:3	What the "day of Jahweh" would mean for Judah
2:4-15	For pagan nations
3:1-8	For Jerusalem
3:9-20	Promise of restoration

The message of Zephaniah is a message of impending doom for Judah and for the surrounding pagan nations. In the spirit of Amos and Isaiah, he appealed to his countrymen to repent while there was still time and hope. Otherwise, the intervention of the Lord would be for them, not deliverance but "a day of wrath, a day of distress and agony, a day of ruin and devastation, a day of darkness and gloom, a day of clouds and blackness, a day of trumpet blast and battle cry" (1:15) (JB).

In our life

Zephaniah's message is brief. But in a few lines he has compressed much of the substance of prophetic teaching on the true nature of religion when he spoke of "the humble and lowly...who seek refuge in God"

172

(cf. 3:12). It is to such as these, "the poor in spirit" as the New Testament would know them, that the kingdom of heaven is offered.

Points to think about

1. Note the lines significant for the theme of the book:
   e.g. the sense of urgency in 1:14-16
         his great word on humility in 2:3
         his emphasis on the holy remnant in 3:12

2. What thoughts would Zephaniah 2:2-3 suggest for today, regarding Christian countries of the West or the world as a whole?

Selections

    1:14—2:3   The day of Jahweh
    3:1-5   Jerusalem, the faithless city
    3:11-18   The humble remnant that will be saved

Prayer: Pray Psalm 90. (JB)
    "You brush men away like waking dreams...."

Song: Draw near, O Lord, our God. (PMB-22)

Thought for the day: Seek the Lord, all you humble of the land who do his commands. Seek righteousness, seek humility (2:3).

HAGGAI

Keeping the faith
in a tedious time

"Because of my house that lies in ruins, while you busy yourselves each with his own house" (1:9b).

The conquest of Babylon by Cyrus in 539 B.C. brought the Babylonian empire to an end. Palestine now became a province of the Persian empire. The Jewish exiles who had returned (cf. Ezr. 1:2-11), had come back home full of enthusiasm. Disillusionment was, however, great and quick. They found the land either devastated or occupied by others. Neighbors looked askance at the new arrivals. So each one had enough to do, taking care of his own affairs, while the "house of the Lord lay in ruins" (Hg. 1:10). In the year 520 B.C., Haggai, together with the prophet Zechariah, roused the people from their lethargy in this regard.

1:1-15	Appeal to rebuild the temple (August 520 B.C.)
2:1-9	The glory that is to come to the temple (October 520 B.C.)
2:10-14	Holiness and "uncleanness" (December 520 B.C.)
2:15-19	A promise of agricultural prosperity
2:20-23	Zerubbabel as Jahweh's servant

In pre-exilic times, the prophets criticized the cult of the times because of the empty dispositions with which it was offered. But now there was neither cult nor temple. The prophet Haggai in his oracles (all reportedly delivered within a four month period in 520 B.C.) roused the people to restore the temple and the cult, which were essential if the people were to become once again a religious community.

174

In the
New Testament

Haggai was convinced that the true foundation of a society's well-being lay in the moral and spiritual order (the temple was to be the outward and visible symbol of this). The New Testament authors share this conviction.

Read Romans 13:1-14.

In the present salvific moment

Today everything seems to be crumbling down all around us. Haggai is a timely encouragement for the builders of the City of God to "keep their faith" in a tedious time.

Points to think about

1. Note the lines which express Haggai's faith:
   (1) In God as the sole master of history
   (2) And the temple as a focal point of messianic hope.

2. The book of Haggai in its present form is more in the nature of a report on the prophet's utterances and the reaction of the people. This would suggest that, in its present form, the prophet himself may not be the author of the book.

3. The prose style of the book of Haggai, whether in the original or in translation, is blunt in comparison with the poetic passages of other prophecies. Yet it is part of the Bible Canon. Life too, is often a compound of poetry and prose. Does this hold a lesson for us as to the possibilities afforded us in life of becoming mature through circumstances?

Selections

1:1-14   Haggai answers the selfish excuses of those who would postpone the work.

2:5-9   The future glory of the temple will exceed that of the first.

Prayer: Psalm 132
This is my resting place for ever.

Song: Like olive branches. Lucien Deiss. (PMB - 159)

Thought for the day: Bring wood and build the house (1:8)

ZECHARIAH

The power
of unrealized hope

"Sing and rejoice, O daughter Zion! See, I am coming to dwell among you, says the Lord" (2:14) (NAB).

Zechariah was a contemporary of the prophet Haggai. With an energy hardly less than that displayed by the latter, Zechariah continued to urge the people to proceed with the work of rebuilding. The reading of this book, however, presents more difficulty to us than the little book of his contemporary. The distance in time that separates us from the prophet's own time has obscured the details of contemporary life and thought that would have facilitated the understanding of the visions in chs. 1-8. And there is the question of the date and authorship (and consequently of the significance) of the latter part of the book, chs. 9-14.

A. The prophet's mission 1:1—8:23
   1. 1:1-6   A call to repentance
   2. 1:7—6:8 The visions of Zechariah
   3. 6:9-15   Zerubbabel symbolically crowned as king-messiah
   4. 7:1—8:23 The enquiry from Bethel about fasting and the reply

B. Messianic panorama 9:1—14:21
   1. 9:1—11:17 The first oracle centered on the Messianic restoration
   2. 12:1—14:21 The second oracle centered on Jerusalem

In line with the prophecy of Haggai, the book of Zechariah expresses the hope of a mysterious return of the former glory of Jerusalem under the co-leadership of the priesthood and the Davidic dynasty. But

177

its vision in the second part seems to extend beyond to messianic times language, when Jahweh's plan and purpose will be finally realized.

In the
New Testament

Although the book of Zechariah presents us with some difficulty, it seems to have had a much greater significance for the Apostolic Church. It is frequently quoted by New Testament authors and writers. See for example:

Mt. 21:5; (Zc. 9)	"The king, meek and riding on an ass."
Mt. 26:15; 27:9-10; (Zc. 11:12)	"The good shepherd priced at thirty pieces of silver."
Mt. 26:31; (Zc. 13:7f.)	"The scattering of the sheep."
Jn. 19:37; (Zc. 1:10f.)	"The transpierced One."
Rv. 6:1-8; (Zc. 1:7f.)	"The four horsemen."
Rv. 11:1-2; 4:10; (Zc. 1:16)	"The measuring of the holy city."
Rv. 11:4-10; (Zc. 4:1-14)	"The 2 olive trees and the lampstands."

Many scholars believe that the influence of Zechariah on the New Testament was even more pervasive than a mere list of quotes would suggest.

In the present salvific moment

The book of Zechariah underlines the idea that the spread of God's truth is really God's work in the final analysis. We are only God's instruments. Perhaps one of the greatest contributions we can make to a hopeless and divided world is to spend all our energies in making God's Word known so that God "will be king of the whole world" (Zc. 14:9).

Points to think about

For various reasons, among them the poor state of the text and the apocalyptic style of writing, Jerome remarked that Zechariah is the most obscure book in the Bible.

— The eight nocturnal visions of Zechariah 1:7—6:8
1. The four horsemen 1:7-17
   —The peace of the empires is coming to an end.
2. The four horns 2:1-4
   —Those who have destroyed Jerusalem will themselves be destroyed.
3. The measurer 2:5-9
   —Jerusalem will be protected.
4. The investiture of the high priest 3:1-10
   —He hails the Messiah.
5. The lampstand and the olive trees 4:1-14
   —The twin powers (spiritual and temporal) at the service of the Lord
6. The scroll of curses 5:1-4
   —The destruction of the impious in Palestine
7. The woman in the ephah (5:5-11)
   —Sin transported to Babylon to draw down punishment there
8. The four chariots that bring destruction (6:1-15)
   —One especially directed against Babylon, the center of the pagan world

2. The difference in style and background between chs. 1-8 on the one hand and chs. 9-14 on the other, have led to the conclusion that these are from different authors and written at different periods. The series of eight visions in part 1 are dated about February, 519 B.C.

The second part possibly dates from the end of the 4th century B.C., when the Persian empire was crumbling down under the blows of the Greeks.

3. It is evident from the context that the original text in 6:11 reads "Zerubbabel" for Joshua, the high priest, who later became head of the community. In fact, the Davidic prince Zerubbabel slips away from history and the prophet's attention is directed toward the temple and the priesthood.

4. Chapter 14 is possibly not from the same hand as 12:1—13:6.

5. Note the lines that particularly emphasize—
    1. God's absolute sovereignty in human affairs.
    2. What God expects of man.

6. Sir Richard W. Livingstone described our age as a "civilization of means without ends." Zechariah's message is that man's only chance to attain the things that really matter lies in being linked with the will and purpose of God.

7. There is a constant struggle in the Old Testament between a narrow and exclusively conceived theocratic nationalism and the idea of the universal reign of God. A comparison of Nahum with Jonah or Ezra with Ruth could illustrate this. The book of Zechariah seems to reach beyond the limited scope of Haggai, reaching to a more pronounced universalism.

"Many nations shall join themselves to the Lord in that day; they shall be my people" (2:15).

Selections

A.	1:1-6	Return to me and I will return to you.
	1:8-17	The vision of the four horsemen (God moves in a mysterious way.)
	6:9-14	A man whose name is branch
B.	9:1-12	The messianic king: his, empire will stretch from sea to sea.

10:3-12 Another Exodus (I mean to bring them back.)

14:1-11 The battle for Jerusalem

Prayer: Psalm 48

His holy mountain, beautiful in elevation, is the joy of all the earth.

Song: Who are these, like stars appearing. T. H. Schenck. (All Saints: 87)

Thought for the day: Many nations shall join themselves to the Lord on that day, and shall be my people (2:11).

MALACHI

A plea for
sincerity in worship

"a pure offering..." (1:11).

The religious fervor of the first years after the return from exile, aroused by the prophets Haggai and Zechariah, had died down. Although apparently the temple had been reconstructed and regular worship resumed (1:7-10), the people of God were no longer truly religious. A sense of frustration and discouragement had set in, accompanied by a degradation in morals and piety on the part of both priests and people. To them, the prophet "Malachi" had something to say that was not only pertinent to the time, but also of abiding value to us.

1:2-5	God's love for Israel
1:6—2:9	An indictment of the priests
2:10-16	Against mixed marriage and divorce
2:17—3:5	The "day of Jahweh" for priests and people
3:6-12	Failure to pay the temple tithes
3:13-21	The just and the unjust on the day of Jahweh
3:22	A Deuteronomic warning (appendix 1)
3:23-24	The return of Elijah (appendix 2)

The message of the book of Malachi is a plea for sincerity in worship in the spirit of Deuteronomy. See 1:7, 8. True cult is not realized by the mere fact of placing one stone upon another. True cult must be the reflection of one's entire life. (Malachi's preaching, in this respect, seems to have prepared the way for the reforms of Ezra and Nehemiah.)

In the
New Testament

The book of Malachi, placed last among the prophetical books (the last in the Old Testament in our English Bibles) ends with a mysterious announcement. The precursor of the "day of Jahweh" already spoken of in Isaiah 40:3, is identified with Elijah (Ml. 3:1, 24). In the New Testament, the text of Malachi is applied to John the Baptist, the precursor of the Messiah, Christ.

Read Matthew 17:1-13.

"I tell you that Elijah has already come and they did not recognize him."

In the present salvific moment

From early times, Christian commentators have seen in "the pure offering" offered to God by the nations "from the rising of the sun to its setting" (1:1, 11), a prophecy of the perfect sacrifice of the messianic age in the Christian Eucharist, the worldwide worship of the Christian Church.

Points to think about

1. It has been suggested that the book of Malachi is an anonymous work since "Malachi" (my messenger) could be a name based on 3:1 rather than a proper name.

2. As you read through the text, highlight the lines that bring out the message of the book of Malachi, e.g., authentic religion (1:7-8)
   responsibility of priests (2:7-8)
   the moral foundations of religion (2:6-7)
   the condemnation of divorce (2:16)
   universal monotheism (1:11-14)
   the precursor of the "day of Jahweh" (3:1, 23-24), etc.

3. For Ml. 3:1, 24, note the following:
   The figure of Elijah, taken up to heaven (2 K. 2:11-13), came to have a considerable role to play in later

apocalyptic thought. His return was to remain an important feature of Jewish eschatology (cf. the book of Enoch) and also in rabbinical literature.

4. Again and again throughout the Old Testament, the sacred authors emphasize the need for sincerity in sacrificial acts (1:7, 8), in ritual and liturgy if religion is to preserve its pristine purity. This is also the lesson of the book of Malachi.

5. Authentic religion has no quarrel with rationality. It is against the cult of irrationality, especially if presented as rationality, that we must continually guard. Hence the need for ministers of religion to keep and guard sound knowledge (2:7).

6. It is the lesson of the Bible that violence among men is often preceded by ingratitude towards and forgetfulness of God (see Gn. 1-11). Permanent peace among men can be achieved only through a brotherhood which derives from the fatherhood of God (cf. Ml. 2:10).

Selections

1:6—2:9; 3:22   Authentic religion and the responsibility of priests

2:17—3:5, 23-24 The "day of Jahweh"

Prayer: Psalm 15
"O Lord, who shall sojourn in your tent?" (NAB)

Song: Wake, awake, the night is dying. Melvin Farrell. (WLSM - A6).

Thought for the day: Have we not all one Father? Did not one God create us? (2:10)

MY FAVORITE PASSAGES FROM THE PROPHETS:

Quiz on the Prophets

1. Who is called the prophet of God's holiness?

2. "Let justice roll down like waters, and righteousness like an everflowing stream."

   Who is the prophet who said these words?

3. Hosea is known as a) the prophet of God's justice.
                        b) the prophet of God's love.
   Mark the correct answer.

4. "Behold the days are coming when I will make a new covenant with the house of Israel."
   Who said these words: Jeremiah or Ezekiel?

5. The shortest book of the prophets is 1) Obadiah
                                        2) Nahum
                                        3) Haggai

6. "Behold, he whose soul is not upright in him shall fail, but the righteous shall live by his faith (or faithfulness)."

   Which prophet said these words?

7. The vision of the valley of dry bones is found in
   a) Daniel
   b) Ezekiel
   Mark the right answer.

8. The promise of the outpouring of the Spirit on all mankind, quoted by Peter at Pentecost, is found in
   a) Zechariah
   b) Joel

9. Which is the book containing the famous prophecy of the Son of Man "coming with the clouds of heaven"?

10. "He has showed you, O man, what is good;
    and what does the Lord require of you
    but to do justice, and to love kindness,
    and to walk humbly with your God?"
    Name the prophet who has said these beautiful lines.

Answers on page 275.

Placing the Books of the Bible in Their Historical Background

There are two ways of doing this.

The first is by answering the question: What is written in the book? (even if it was written after the event).

The second by answering the question: When was it written? (However, one has to remember that a certain number of books of the Bible were composed little by little through the centuries.)

In the following table,
the first column recalls the main periods,
the second and third columns help answer the above questions. (The classification is not exhaustive.)

The Main Periods or Stages (Approx. Dates)	Books That Tell About These Periods or Stages	Some Books That Were Actually Written Down in These Periods
The Stage Setting	The beginning of the world and pre-history.	Genesis 1-11	(Before writing, Israel lived, prayed, struggled and transmitted orally.)
1 - 1800-1250 The first steps in salvation history: The Patriarchal Period.	Genesis 12-50	
2 - 1250-1200 The birth of a nation: The Exodus.	Ex.-Dt.-Nb.-Lv.	
3 - 1200-1020 The Promised Land.	Jos.-Jg.-Rt.	
4 - 1020-932 The Monarchy (Golden Age with David and Solomon).	1 and 2 Samuel 1 K. 1-10	1 and 2 Samuel (in part). 1 K. 1-10 (in part).
5 - 932-587 A divided people. Decadence	1 K. 11 – 2 K. 25 1 and 2 Ch.	Certain chs. of Gn. and Ex.

187

The Main Periods or Stages (Approx. Dates)	The Books That Speak to Us About These Periods	The Books That Were Written in These Periods
c. 750 740	Amos (in the northern Kingdom) Hosea (north) Isaiah (south) Micah (south)	Amos, Hosea Isaiah 1-39 Micah
End of N. Kingdom 721 701 650 627	Last words of Isaiah Zephaniah Jeremiah	1st collections of Proverbs Zephaniah Jeremiah
Religious reform of 622 612 600	Nahum Habakkuk	Nahum Habakkuk
End of S. Kingdom 587		
6 - 587-538	End of Jer., Lam.	Lamentations, Ezekiel
The Exile: A "peak-experience" for the People of God	Ezk., prophet of the exile. Obadiah	Re-editing of some books of the Bible. Lv., 1 and 2 Kings, Gn. 1-12, Isaiah 40-55, 1 and 2 Chronicles, Ezra and Nehemiah, Isaiah 56-66
538 The return	Ezra and Nehemiah	

7 - A long period of waiting (under foreign domination) Persian period (538-333)	Haggai, Zechariah Joel Malachi	Haggai, Zechariah 1-8 Joel Collection of Psalms finished. Collection of Proverbs completed. Song of Solomon, Job, Jonah, Ruth
Greek period (333-63)	(No book for the beginning) Daniel 1 and 2 Maccabees	Baruch, Qoheleth, Zechariah 9-14, Tobit, Esther, Judith, Daniel, 1 and 2 Maccabees, Sirach (Ecclesiasticus) Wisdom
8 - Roman period (63- Christ: God with us (7 B.C.— c 30 A.D.)	Gospel acc. Mt., Mk., Lk., Jn.	
9 - **The Church** The Church in Palestine Conversion of Paul 36-37 Beyond Palestine	Acts of the Apostles Galatians	Apostolic witness of the resurrection: their life and preaching, the oral Gospel. At the beginning, nothing written)

Date / Event		Documents
		1st written documents of the N.T.
52		1 Thessalonians
		2 Thessalonians, Galatians
54-57	Corinthians, Romans, etc.	1 Corinthians, 2 Corinthians
57-58		Romans, James
Paul prisoner at Rome		Philippians
61-62		Colossians, Ephesians
65-67	2 Timothy	Philemon, 1 Peter
		Titus
Martyrdom of Peter and Paul c. 67		1 and 2 Timothy, Hebrews,
		Gospel according to Mark
Jerusalem destroyed 70 A.D.		Gospel according to Matthew
70-80		Gospel according to Luke, Acts of the Apostles
		Jude, 1 John
95		2 and 3 John
		Final edition of Gospel according to John
"To the ends of the earth"		Revelation, 2 Peter

"And know that I am with you always; yes to the end of time" (Mt. 28:20) (JB).

190

The New Testament

"In many and various ways God spoke of old to our fathers by the prophets; but in these last days he has spoken to us by a Son..." (Heb. 1:1-2).

As we went through the pages of the Old Testament, we tried to trace the gradual development of God's plan for man's salvation. We now turn to the New Testament where this plan reaches its fulfillment in God's saving work in the life and preaching of Jesus Christ, God made man, culminating in His death and resurrection: the Paschal Mystery. The Gospels and the Acts present this to us, and the Epistles explain it and apply it to our daily lives.

THE GOSPEL
ACCORDING TO MATTHEW

"The kingdom of heaven is at hand" (3:2).

An ancient tradition regards Matthew as the first of the Gospel writers. This probably accounts for the position of Matthew as the first Gospel in the New Testament (although Mark is generally admitted by modern scholars to be the earliest of the four Gospels as we have them today in Greek). Jewish Christians in Palestine and elsewhere were having a difficult time coping with Jewish unbelief and hostility. This circumstance appears to form the background of Matthew's Gospel.

Chs. 1-2 The preparation of the kingdom in the person of the Child-Messiah

3-7 The formal proclamation of the kingdom to the disciples and the public
 A. Chs. 3-4 Narrative section
 B. Chs. 5-7 The discourse setting forth the new spirit of the kingdom

8-10 The preaching of the kingdom: "signs confirming the Word";
 A. Chs. 8-9 Mainly narrative; 10 miracles of Jesus
 B. Ch. 10 Apostolic discourse; the apostles chosen and sent to preach the word.

11-13 The kingdom of God is not according to human expectation: hence it meets with obstacles and resistance (chs. 11-12 are mainly narrative. Ch. 13 has the same idea presented in parables).

14-18 Embryonic realization of the kingdom in the Church established by Christ: the little group of disciples with Peter as its head.

A. Ch. 14-17 Mainly narrative
B. Ch. 18   Short discourse on the rules that are to govern the community (humility, good example, prayer, love and forgiveness).

19-25 Crisis: Increasing hostility of the Jewish leaders; an eschatological kingdom
A. 19-23   Mainly narrative (and a few parables)
B. 24 and 25 Concluding eschatological discourse

Chs. 26-28 Passion and resurrection: triumph in failure
Concludes with mission to the entire world.

Matthew's Gospel has often been called the Gospel of the kingdom or the Gospel of the Church. It was to establish the kingdom of God, promised by the prophets, that Christ came. He did this by the Paschal event of His death and resurrection and establishing the Church, the kingdom of God on earth, the New Israel.

In the
Old Testament

The central theme of Matthew's Gospel seems to be to show that the Old Testament is fulfilled in the New. Care is taken to show how the kingdom of heaven was prepared in the Old Testament, foretold and fulfilled in greater perfection in the New Testament. Christ is presented as a second and greater Moses, who repeats the Law but corrects it and raises it to heights undreamed of in the Old Testament (Mt. 5:21-28).

In our life

The beatitudes of the sermon on the Mount outline a whole program of Christian life. They are meant for every Christian, not only for a select few. They are a program to which one must continually return. For it is there that the kingdom of heaven is. "Happy are...for theirs is the kingdom of heaven"; these beatitudes judge the quality of our life and of our actions.

Points to think about

1. Matthew speaks of "the kingdom" some 52 times in his Gospel. We are all called to this kingdom, and to work for its increase in the hearts of men. All men, at some time or other in their lives, have to choose for or against it. In the eschatological discourse and the parables of chapters 24 and 25, Matthew shows the rejection of the greater part of the Chosen People, because they were not ready for the kingdom, and the substitution by God of a New People of God. It is a matter of being ready.

2. Note how the five great discourses in Matthew end with a similar conclusion (7:28; 11:1; 13:53; 19:1; 26:1). Because of this, this Gospel is frequently presented as being composed of five "booklets" after the manner of the Pentateuch, which contained the Law of Moses. As you read Matthew, it is good to see how all through his Gospel, he shows that Jesus realizes the expectation of Israel. Highlight or note all the citations of the Old Testament (they are usually in a different print).

3. According to many modern scholars, the Gospel of Matthew was written probably after the destruction of Jerusalem in 70 A.D. According to Origen, Jerome and others, the readers for whom the Gospel was intended were Christians who came from Judaism. The vocabulary used is typically Palestinian. (In fact, some think of a possible shorter Aramaic "Gospel" of Matthew which preceded this Greek one we have today. The latter, however, is not thought to be a mere translation of the former, but an adaptation or a new work.) Further,

Palestinian customs are frequently mentioned without explanation (unlike in Mark and Luke).

4. Note that Matthew, like Luke, gives us some account of the infancy of Jesus. (Mark does not, but begins with the preaching of John the Baptist and the baptism of Jesus, as is also the case with the discourses in the Acts of the Apostles.) The infancy narratives are meant as a reflection upon and an introduction to the "mystery of Jesus."

A question often asked about these narratives, both in Matthew and Luke, is: to what extent are they historically accurate? It is difficult to answer such a question in a few lines. Suffice it to note that besides the fact that a period of nearly sixty or seventy years separates them from the events of which they speak, they are written in a literary form somewhat different from the narratives of the public life of Jesus, beginning with His baptism. The infancy narratives are deeply theological. Luke is particularly so. These narratives have accordingly to be seen through the eyes of the mother of Jesus (Mary was with the apostles after the ascension, as we note in Ac. 1:14), those of the disciples and the first Christian community. It is the sharing of a look of faith (as in the canticles of Mary, Zechariah and Simeon in Luke), of the post-resurrection faith of the apostolic church.

Selections

Ch. 5	The inaugural proclamation of the kingdom
13:1-32	The nature of the kingdom in parables
22-23	A series of controversies with the pharisees
25:1-13	Who will inherit the kingdom?

Prayer: Recite Mt. 6:9-13
     Our Father who art in heaven.

Song: Blessed are the pure in heart. Gregory Norbert. (LWH - 9)

Thought for the day: Father in heaven, may Your kingdom come.

THE GOSPEL ACCORDING TO MARK

Who is
this man?

"The gospel of Jesus Christ, the Son of God" (1:1).

In Mark's Gospel, we seem to find the traditional preaching of the apostle Peter (Mark was Peter's assistant in the apostolate) augmented with material gathered from other authentic sources. Thus, Mark's Gospel is a faithful account of the life and teaching of Jesus, as attested to by the witnesses of the first generation Church and according to many scholars presents the primitive proclamation, in its simplicity, as no other Gospel does.

Chs.	1:1-13	Introduction: the prelude
	1:14—7:23	The ministry in Galilee
	7:24—10:52	Ministry outside Galilee
	11-13	In Jerusalem
	14-16	The passion and resurrection

In reading the Gospel of Mark, one almost has the impression of walking at the side of Peter through the villages, the roads, the hills and valleys of Palestine, recalling to mind, all the time, anecdotes and words of Jesus connected with these places. Yet a reflective reading shows it has deeper dimensions: it is penetrated through and through with the mystery surrounding the person of Jesus of Nazareth. The first section of the Gospel (1:14—8:30) appears as the answer to the question: who is this man? The Messiah. And the second part as answer to the question: What kind of Messiah? The mysterious "Son of Man."

In the
Old Testament

Mark's Gospel brings out a notable difference between the Old Testament and the New. The Old Testament, for the most part, can be said to recount the history of a people, the people of Israel. In the New Testament, the story is primarily about a Person, as the opening lines of Mark have it: "The beginning of the gospel of Jesus Christ, the Son of God" (1:1).

In our life

The liturgy of the Church has no other aim but to bring us into vital contact with the mystery of Christ. The reading of Mark's Gospel helps us, when at the liturgy (Sunday Mass, for example), to fix our gaze on Christ, God Incarnate, and to ask for a faith like that of Peter, whose faith in this respect must have shone out in his preaching.

Points to think about

1. A recurring idea in Mark's Gospel is the "Messianic secret" (or the strange unwillingness of Jesus to manifest Himself openly as Messiah). We know that the Jews expected a victorious and triumphant Messiah. So Jesus could not reveal Himself as Messiah to them without danger of being misunderstood. The mystery of suffering in Christ's life had to be fully revealed only by the Easter event.

2. Mark follows closely the Semitic usages and style of speaking of the people, the style of speaking of Peter, the fisherman of the lake of Tiberias. Scenes are described in the present as they occurred, with "everyday" words, and often without much logical connection.

3. Who exactly was Mark? He is surnamed also John-Mark, not one of the twelve. But he takes part with his cousin Barnabas in the first missions of Paul. Then he separates himself from Paul (see Acts 13:13 and 15:36-

40) to find him again later when Paul is in prison (Col. 4:10, Phm. 24). He has close links with Peter (1 P. 5:13). Papias of Herapolis, writing about 110 A.D. and quoting his master, "John the elder," said: "Mark, the interpreter of Peter, who wrote accurately, but not in order, all that he recalled of the words or actions of the Lord."

4. Regarding the date of Mark's Gospel and its intended readers: internal criticism would indicate a date before 70 A.D. (the date of the destruction of Jerusalem), possibly between 65-70 A.D. It was plainly intended for Christians of non-Jewish origin living outside Palestine, perhaps Gentile Christian readers in Rome.

5. The Gospel of Mark, as we have it in our English Bibles today, ends with a significant remark. All Christians are sent into the entire world to proclaim the Good News. Although they are "sent," they are not alone; the Lord is "working with them." So it is today also.

6. If you read attentively Peter's discourse to the Gentiles at Cornelius' "baptism" (Acts 10:34-43), you will see that it contains, as it were, the broad outlines of the Gospel of Mark.

Selections

Chs. 1:1-11	Introduction: John the baptizer and Jesus of Nazareth
2:1-12	Jesus' power to forgive sins
4:35-41	Jesus, Lord of nature
8:27—9:13	The mysterious Son of man

Prayer: Recite Psalm 2
   You are my son, today I have begotten you.

Song: There was a man named John the Baptist. Gregory Norbert. (LWH - 1)

Thought for the day: "Repent, and believe the Good News" (1:15) (JB).

THE GOSPEL ACCORDING TO LUKE

Joy to
the world

"Glory to God in high heaven, peace on earth to those on whom his favor rests" (2:14) (NAB).

The "Good News" that was Christianity was spreading rapidly throughout the Roman empire, finding adherents almost everywhere and in every class of society. The Roman authorities began to view Christianity with hostility, particularly since Nero's persecution of the Christians (c. A.D. 64-68) as scapegoats for the burning of Rome. Luke, a Gentile by birth and missionary companion of the "Apostle of the Gentiles," wrote his Gospel to show the world that Christianity was not a kind of subversive movement but a world-religion of peace and joy, transcending in its universality all races and national limitations.

Now open your Bible and read: The Gospel according to Luke.

Prologue	1:1-4	
Infancy	1:5—2:52	
and		Note how the canticles bring out
childhood		the deeper meaning of the narrative.
The ministry in Galilee	3:1—9:50	
	3:1—4:13	Preaching of John, baptism, temptation (Introduction)
	4:14—6:11	Nazareth, Capernaum, call of disciples, miracles
	6:12—8:3	Choice of the twelve, discourse, miracles
	8:4—9:50	Parables, miracles
Ministry outside Galilee (on the "way to Jerusalem")	9:51—19:27	
	9:51—13:21	Samaria, mission of the 70, sayings, controversies, etc.

       13:22—17:10 More sayings, controversies, parables

       17:11—19:27 Miracles, discourses, parables, Zacchaeus, etc.

Ministry in Jerusalem   19:28—21:38
The Passion   22:1—23:56
The resurrection narratives   ch. 24

One of the great themes of Luke's Gospel is that of the universality of salvation, namely that the good news of the Gospel, the good news of the joy of salvation is for all men, for Gentile and Jew, for men and women, for sinner and saint, for rich and poor. Luke's Gospel is truly the "Good News" of joy to the whole world.

In the Old Testament

Throughout the pages of the Old Testament, Jerusalem had a special significance. The fate of Jerusalem and those of the people of God were closely linked. Luke, too, makes Jerusalem the pivotal point of his Gospel (it begins and ends in Jerusalem). It is there that the culminating act of the history of salvation was enacted. This role was to pass to the New Jerusalem, the Church, spread over the entire world, as the prophets had foretold.

Read: Isaiah 2:1-4; 19:19-22; 60:1-6.

In our life

The Gospel of Luke has been called the Gospel of joy. One finds it everywhere in Luke. The early Christians too were filled with this joy in the Holy Spirit. The more one's life becomes authentically Christian, and filled with the Holy Spirit, the more it will abound in this joy.

Points to think about

1. Note how Luke is careful to preserve the threefold plan already established in Mark: Galilee, journeys,

Jerusalem. Note also the difference. There is much more in Luke (9:51—18:14 are found only in Luke). Further, Luke does not merely tell us what he knows to be true, he presents it with art.

2. Luke's Gospel is also more "theological" than Mark's; in fact, he is the most theological of the three synoptic Gospels. Mark's Gospel has been called a "pre-resurrection Gospel," but Luke, right from the beginning, focuses the light on the mystery of the death-resurrection events on the whole life of Jesus. Already in the infancy narratives, he introduces us straightway into the Old Testament milieu and shows how the announcement of the birth of the Savior is the beginning of the fulfillment of God's plan of salvation begun with Abraham.

3. Luke's Gospel is pervaded by the spirit of joy, of prayer, of compassion, of self-denial. In particular, his insistence on prayer and the internal link between joy and self-renunciation make Luke's Gospel very relevant for the world of today. In fact, in Luke, Jesus demands an absolute renunciation on the part of those who would follow him (see 6:34-35; 12:13, 21, 33; 13:23; 14:12-14, 25-33; 16:9-13, etc.). Further, this life of following Christ is possible only in a deep union with Him by prayer. Christ Himself has given us an example in this in the great moments of His life, e.g., at His baptism, 3:21; choice of the apostles, 6:12; at the transfiguration, 9:28. In Luke, Christ loves to draw apart by Himself to pray (6:16). He teaches us how to pray (11:1, 5-10; 18:1-5, 10-14, etc.).

4. Another factor that makes Luke's Gospel relevant today and in all times is the place he gives to the Holy Spirit in the economy of salvation. Not only in the infancy narratives, but also on all important occasions in the life of Jesus, we find mention of the Holy Spirit (cf. for example, 4:14-18, 10:21). The Spirit is especially the presence of Jesus continued in our world (cf. 24:49). As you read Luke, it is worth highlighting some of these passages. Perhaps it would be one way of better

discovering the Holy Spirit in our life. See 1:15, 35, 41, 67; 2:25-27; 3:16, 22; 4:1, 14, 18; 10:21; 11:13; 12:10, 12; etc.

5. One of the things that we need to know most is the goodness of the Lord. Luke shows the goodness of Christ in a remarkable way. Christ keeps company with sinners (15:1-2), He pardons the sinner (7:36-50), the rich publican Zacchaeus (19:1-10), His executioners (23:34), the thief and robber (23:39-43). He goes after the lost sheep (15:4-7), and weeps over Jerusalem (19:41-44). The return of the sinner would be an occasion of joy for all (15:7, 10, 24, 32).

6. Luke speaks of Mary, the mother of Jesus, in such a way as to show her place in the economy of salvation. The passages in this respect in the document of Vatican II "Lumen gentium" (Dogmatic Constitution on the Church)[1] can be linked to the Gospels by Luke's beautiful narrative of the annunciation and Mary's canticle, the Magnificat. In the Church, Mary is the model of the believer in whom God can do great things.

Note also how Luke takes care to underline Mary's personal sanctity. More than any one else in the Old Testament or New Testament, she is the object of God's special grace and favor, and in her the messianic hopes of the Old Testament reach fulfillment. See 1:28, 30, 35, 42-49. Also 2:19f., 34.

7. Regarding the destination of the Gospel, its literary characteristics leave no doubt that it is the work of a Gentile Christian and written for Gentile Christians and the Gentile world. Regarding the date, however, there is no firm tradition. Some place it around 70 A.D.; others, even after 80 A.D.

---

1. See **Dogmatic Constitution on the Church** of the Second Vatican Council, ch. 8, especially nos. 55-59.

Selections
   2:10-20 The good news of joy to the whole world
   10:25-37 Who is my neighbor?'
   14:15-24 For whom is the kingdom?
   15:11-32 God's pardon
   18:18-30 The cost of discipleship

Prayer: The canticle of Zechariah (1:68-79)
   "...to give light to those who sit in darkness and in the shadow of death."

   O God, by the message of an angel, You made known the Incarnation of Your Son. Grant that through His passion and cross, we may attain the glory of His resurrection. Through the same Christ, our Lord. Amen.

Song: The goodness of God cries out. Gregory Norbert. (LWH - 2)

Thought for the day: "If any man would come after me, let him deny himself and take up his cross daily and follow me" (Lk. 9:23).

GOSPEL ACCORDING TO JOHN

> And the Word became flesh
> and dwelt among us (1:14).

In a way somewhat different from the other Gospel writers, John has his own presentation of the person and the work of the Lord. The over-all purpose in writing his Gospel seems to be to explain, as it were, the total meaning of the life of Christ. In his prologue, he takes his readers outside of time to the eternal pre-existence of the Word with God, and in this background he underlines the deeper significance of the words and deeds of Christ, seen in all their depth.

A. 1. The prologue. 1:1-18
   2. The beginnings. 1:19—4:54

1:19-51	The testimony of John the baptizer and the call of the first disciples
2:1—3:36	The first sign at Cana, the cleansing of the temple, Nicodemus, testimony of John the baptizer
4:1-42	Jesus in Samaria
4:43-54	The 2nd sign: the healing of the ruler's son at Capernaum

   3. The ministry of Jesus. 5:1—10:39

5:1-47	The 3rd sign: the cure of the paralytic and the debate
6:1-71	The 4th sign: the miracle of the loaves and the discourse on the Eucharist
7:1-52	Discourse and debate at Jerusalem
7:53—8:11	The adulterous woman
8:12-59	Discourse and debate on the light
9:1-41	Cure of the man born blind

Like the synoptic writers, John is also writing history, but it is history seen in all its theological and spiritual dimensions. He not only recounts the words and actions of Jesus, but also explains their meaning. Since the whole work is inspired, we can see in John's explanations the action of the Holy Spirit bringing out the deeper and fuller significance of Christ's life, His words and deeds among men.

In the
Old Testament

John's Gospel needs to be read in the background of the life and institutions of the people of God in the Old Testament. For example, the sanctuary of Christ's body was spoken of in terms of the temple at Jerusalem (Jn. 2:19), and the salvific value of Christ's death on the cross was symbolized by the brazen serpent of Moses in the desert (Jn. 3:14). The feeding of the multitude points forward to the Eucharist of the Church symbolized by the manna in the desert (6:31). Jesus is Himself the good shepherd spoken of by the prophets (cf. Jn. ch. 10).

Read Ezekiel 34:7-24.

In our life

The Gospel of John is the Gospel for us of today, for it shows Christ as eternally present and acting in and through His Church and her sacraments, especially Baptism and the Eucharist. Through these, the redeeming grace of the historic events that took place in Palestine are extended to men down the centuries. He seems to say to us: you need not look back to the past. Live right now the life of the Risen Jesus through His Spirit in the Church of the living God.

Points to think about

1. In reading the Gospel of John, the main thing is to keep in mind the meaning of the Gospel as noted above. The division given above helps to know the contents of the Gospel as such. Another division adopted by scholars is the following:

A. 1:19—12:50 **The Book of Signs**
   Note the signs by way of words
6:35	The Bread of Life
8:12	The Light of the world
8:58	Before Abraham was, I am
10:9	The Door
10:11	The Good Shepherd
11:25	The Resurrection and the Life
14:6	The Way, the Truth, the Life
15:1	The true Vine

   Other signs by way of works
2:1-11	Changing of water into wine
2:13-22	Cleansing of the Temple
4:46-54	Healing of the son of the nobleman

2. Note how the prologue of John 1:1-18 is like a summary of the whole Gospel. Like the overture of a symphony, it touches on the principal themes of the revelation and the reactions it would provoke. It could be divided into three strophes.

The paschal prayer of Jesus in ch. 17 once again reverts to the same perspective. Now it is the return of Jesus to the Father through the passion and the cross and resurrection.

3. As noted above, perhaps the most important thing is to perceive in the Gospel of John how he is more concerned than the other three evangelists to bring out the significance of the events of Christ's life, of His words and deeds. The words of Christ, for John, had a deeper meaning not perceived at the time, but which would be fully understood only after His glorification. The dialogue with Nicodemus, for instance (3:1-21), throws much light on the meaning of Baptism, and

chapter 6 on the meaning of the Eucharist, etc. In this way, the words of Christ are seen as directly related to a Christian's daily life.

4. John underlines, in particular, the existential choice that all men have constantly to make in their lives, the choice between the light and the darkness, the "yes" and the "no" to the call of God (6:60-71). Perhaps more than any other evangelist the reading and re-reading of John, in faith, puts us in vital contact with the one Person who reveals the Father to us, Christ, the Son of the living God, and demands that we make this choice in a total commitment of our whole being to God in Jesus Christ.

Selections

1:1-18   The Word was made flesh.
8:31-58 Before Abraham ever was, I am.
14:1-21 The Way, the Truth, the Life
17:1-11 Back to the Father

Prayer: Recite John 17:1-11, 24-26.
"That they may be one, even as we are one."
O Lord, Jesus Christ, You are the Way, the Truth, and the Life. We ask You not to let us stray from You, who are the Way, nor to distrust You, who are the Truth, nor to rest in any other thing than You, who are the Life. Teach us by Your Holy Spirit what to believe, what to do, and wherein to take our rest. For Your own name's sake we ask it. Amen (Desiderius Erasmus, 16th century).

Song: You, Lord, are the Way. Lucien Deiss. (BHP, II 76)

Thought for the day: I am the Way, the Truth and the Life (14:6).

An over-all view of the four Gospels

1. The four Gospels at a glance

	MARK	MATTHEW	LUKE	JOHN
1. Theme underlined	The person of Jesus	Fulfillment of the Old Testament (the Church)	Universality of salvation	The total meaning of the life of Jesus
2. First intended probably for:	The non-Jews (Gentiles) in Rome	Jews in Palestine (Syria? Caesarea?)	The Gentile world	First and second generation Christians (in Asia Minor? everywhere?)
3. Probable date written	Late 60's A.D.	Early 70's A.D.	Sometime around 70 A.D.	Final redaction in the 80's or 90's
4. Probable place written	Rome	Somewhere in Palestine. Antioch in Syria?	Rome	Ephesus?

2. Miracles in the Gospels (a comparison)

a. Common to all the evangelists

1. The feeding of the five thousand — Mk. 6:34f., Mt. 14:15f., Lk. 9:10f., Jn. 6:1f.

b. Common to Mark, Matthew, Luke

1. The healing of a leper — Mk. 1:40f., Mt. 8:2f., Lk. 5:12f.
2. The healing of Peter's mother-in-law — Mk. 1:30f., Mt. 8:14f., Lk. 4:38f.
3. Calming the tempest — Mk. 4:37f., Mt. 8:23f., Lk. 8:22f.
4. The Gadarene demoniacs — Mk. 5:1f., Mt. 8:28f., Lk. 8:26f.
5. The healing of the paralytic — Mk. 2:1f., Mt. 9:2f., Lk. 5:18f.
6. Jairus' daughter — Mk. 5:23f., Mt. 9:18f., Lk. 8:41f.

    7. The woman with a   Mk. 5:25f., Mt. 9:20f.,
       hemorrhage   Lk. 8:43f.
    8. The epileptic boy   Mk. 9:14f., Mt. 17:14f.,
                           Lk. 9:37f.
    9. The man with the   Mk. 3:1f., Mt. 12:10f.,
       withered hand   Lk. 6:6f.
   10. Bartimaeus, the   Mk. 10:46f., Mt. 20:30f.,
       blind man   Lk. 18:35f.

c. Common to Mark, Matthew, John
    1. The walking on the Mk. 6:45f., Mt. 14:22f.,
       water   Jn. 6:16f.

d. Common to Mark and Matthew
    1. The Canaanite
       woman's daughter   Mk. 7:24f., Mt. 15:21f.
    2. Feeding of the four
         thousand   Mk. 8:1f., Mt. 15:32f.
    3. The barren fig tree   Mk. 11:13-14, Mt. 21:19f.

e. Common to Mark and Luke
    1. The demoniac in
       the synagogue of
       Capernaum   Mk. 1:23f., Lk. 4:33f.

f. Common to Matthew and Luke
    1. The centurion's
       servant   Mt. 8:4f., Lk. 7:1f.
    2. Jesus and
       Beelzebub   Mt. 12:22f., Lk. 11:14f.

g. Found only in Mark
    1. The deaf mute   Mk. 7:31-37
    2. The blind man of
       Bethsaida   Mk. 8:22-26

h. Found only in Matthew
    1. Cure of two blind
       men   Mt. 9:27-31

2. The dumb
    demoniac   Mt. 9:32-34
3. Tax money in the
    mouth of the fish   Mt. 17:24-27

i. Found only in Luke
    1. The miraculous
        catch of fish   Lk. 5:1-11
    2. The widow's son at
        Naim   Lk. 7:11-17
    3. The woman with
        a spirit which
        drained her
        strength   Lk. 13:11-17
    4. The man with
        dropsy   Lk. 14:1-6f.
    5. The ten lepers   Lk. 17:11-19
    6. Healing of
        Malchus' ear   Lk. 22:50-51

j. Found only in John
    1. Water made wine
        at Cana   Jn. 2:1-11
    2. Cure of the noble-
        man's son of fever   Jn. 4:46-54
    3. The man born
        blind   Jn. 9:1-7
    4. The resurrection of
        Lazarus   Jn. 11:1-44
    5. Catch of fish by
        the sea of Tiberias Jn. 21:1-14

3. Parables in the Gospels (a comparison)

    a. Common to Mark, Matthew and Luke
        1. The lamp on the   Mk. 4:21-22, Mt. 5:14-16,
            lampstand   Lk. 8:16-17
        2. The sewing of new
            cloth on old   Mk. 2:21, Mt. 9:16,
            garments   Lk. 5:36

3. New wine in old   Mk. 2:22, Mt. 9:17,
   wineskins   Lk. 5:37-38
4. The sower   Mk. 4:13-20; Mt. 13:3-9,
                        18-23; Lk. 8:4-15
5. The mustard seed   Mk. 4:30-32, Mt.
                        13:31-32, Lk. 13:18-19
6. The vineyard and   Mk. 12:1-11, Mt.
   husbandmen   21:33-46, Lk. 20:9-19
7. Young leaves of the Mk. 13:28-32, Mt. 24:32-
   fig tree   36, Lk. 21:29-33

b. Common to Matthew and Luke
1. House built on the
   rock   Mt. 7:24-27, Lk. 6:47-49
2. The leaven   Mt. 13:33, Lk. 13:20-21
3. The lost sheep   Mt. 18:12-14, Lk. 15:3-7

c. Found only in Mark
1. The blade, the ear,
   the full grain   Mk. 4:26-29
2. Watch for His
   coming!   Mk. 13:33-36

d. Found only in Matthew
 1. The weeds   Mt. 13:24-30
 2. The hidden
    treasure   Mt. 13:44
 3. The pearl of great
    price   Mt. 13:45-46
 4. The dragnet   Mt. 13:47-48
 5. The unmerciful
    servant   Mt. 18:23-35
 6. Laborers in the
    vineyard   Mt. 20:1-16
 7. The two sons   Mt. 21:28-32
 8. The wedding feast   Mt. 22:1-14
 9. The ten virgins   Mt. 25:1-13
10. The talents   Mt. 25:14-30
11. The sheep and
    the goats   Mt. 25:31-46

e. Found only in Luke

1. The two debtors	Lk. 7:36-50
2. The good Samaritan	Lk. 10:25-37
3. The importunate friend	Lk. 11:5-8
4. The rich fool	Lk. 12:13-21
5. The watchful servants	Lk. 12:35-40
6. The wise steward	Lk. 12:42-48
7. The barren fig tree	Lk. 13:6-9
8. The great banquet	Lk. 14:15-24
9. The tower and the cost	Lk. 14:28-33
10. The lost sheep	Lk. 15:3-7
11. The lost coin	Lk. 15:8-10
12. The prodigal son	Lk. 15:11-32
13. The unjust steward	Lk. 16:1-8
14. The rich man and Lazarus	Lk. 16:19-31
15. The master and the servant	Lk. 17:7-10
16. The importunate widow	Lk. 18:1-8
17. The pharisee and the publican	Lk. 18:9-14
18. The ten units of money	Lk. 19:11-27 [1]

[1] To make similar comparisons, see:

Xavier Leon-DuFour, **Concordance of the Synoptic Gospels**, tr. R. O'Connell (N.Y.: Desclée, 1957). In this book, by a clever use of columns, the author makes pleasant and easy the comparison between the texts and their inter-relations.

A. T. Robertson, **A Harmony of the Gospels** (N.Y.: Harper & Row, 1950).

Burton H. Throckmorton, Jr., ed., **Gospel Parallels,** A Synopsis of the First Three Gospels (Camden, N.J.: T. Nelson & Sons, 1967).

4. The synoptic question: Mark, Matthew and Luke

Matthew, Mark and Luke have been called the synoptic Gospels because of their similarity of outlook. Numerous agreements between them argue for a certain literary interdependence, while numerous divergences, additions and omissions indicate a certain literary independence. The question of their relations with one another and their origins is called the synoptic question and has occupied the minds of scholars especially since the late 18th century:

A. Some facts: (1) Mark has 677 verses; Matthew 1070 and Luke 1150.

(2) Mark has about 70 verses out of his 677 proper to himself, Matthew about 330 and Luke about 520.

(3) Some texts are common to Mark, Matthew and Luke (between 350-370 verses).

(4) Some texts are common only to two of the synoptics. To Mark and Matthew between 170-180 verses; to Mark and Luke between about 50 verses; to Matthew and Luke about 230 verses.

(5) It is generally admitted that the present Mark is more primitive than the present Matthew and Luke. (Mark's brevity and other features of style strongly support this.)

B. With the chronological background, the formation of the Gospels would look roughly like this:

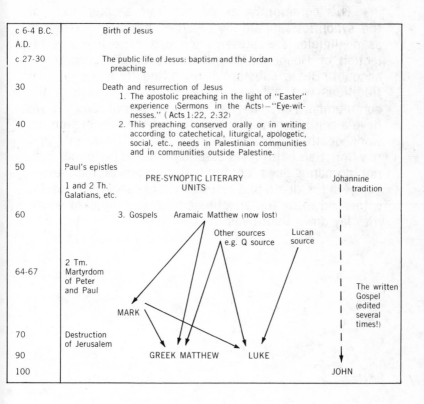

c 6-4 B.C. A.D.		Birth of Jesus	
c 27-30		The public life of Jesus: baptism and the Jordan preaching	
30		Death and resurrection of Jesus 1. The apostolic preaching in the light of "Easter" experience (Sermons in the Acts)—"Eye-witnesses." (Acts 1:22, 2:32)	
40		2. This preaching conserved orally or in writing according to catechetical, liturgical, apologetic, social, etc., needs in Palestinian communities and in communities outside Palestine.	
50	Paul's epistles 1 and 2 Th. Galatians, etc.	PRE-SYNOPTIC LITERARY UNITS	Johannine tradition
60		3. Gospels Aramaic Matthew (now lost) Other sources e.g. Q source Lucan source	
64-67	2 Tm. Martyrdom of Peter and Paul	MARK	The written Gospel (edited several times!)
70	Destruction of Jerusalem		
90		GREEK MATTHEW LUKE	
100			JOHN

C. The historical value of the Gospels—or the question: Do we reach the Jesus of history through the Gospels of our New Testament?

In trying to answer this question, perhaps the most important factor to keep in mind is the nature of the primitive Christian community. This Christian community was not an amorphous multitude but a community with a structure. There were eye-witnesses in charge of the preservation and transmission of the recollections (see Acts 1:22, 2:32). This contributed in great measure to preserving the traditions from any substantial change from what Jesus actually did and taught.

This community, as we see from a comparison of the synoptics, apparently regarded minute divergences as negligible. The presentation was more like a recollection (cf. Gospel of Mark) than a report or stenographic account. But a substantial departure from the original traditions was not easy because of the nature of the community. Thus, we can say that in our Gospels we have a solid historical substratum of the life, preaching, work, death and resurrection of Jesus of Nazareth, and the Christian Faith rests essentially on an historical fact, not primarily on a doctrine—the historical fact, especially, of the death and resurrection of Jesus of Nazareth, witnessed to by the apostles and in testimony of which they lay down their lives.

THE ACTS OF THE APOSTLES

"To the end of the earth" (1:8)

The Acts of the Apostles is the second book written by Luke. In his first, his Gospel, he had shown the beginning of Messianic times and how Christ had laid the foundation of the New Israel, the New People of God, who were to be built up. In the Acts, he shows the actual birth of this Church and how it increased first in Palestine and then throughout the then-known world. The Acts give us precious insights into the life of this early Church and the activity, particularly of the two great apostles, Peter and Paul.

1:1-11	Prologue
1:12—5:42	The first period of the Christian community in Jerusalem
6—12	The first missions
13:1—15:35	The mission of Barnabas and Paul: The Council of Jerusalem
15:36—19:20	The missions of Paul
19:21—28:29	Paul, a prisoner for Christ

Although this second part of Luke's work records the acts of the apostles, the real "hero" of the work is the Holy Spirit. It is He who makes the apostles begin their mission on Pentecost. And later, at each moment of crisis in the growth of the Church, it is His intervention that decides the issue and guides the Church in her mission of spreading the Good News. In a word, it's the Holy Spirit who plays the decisive role in the Acts of the Apostles.

In the Old Testament

One of the characteristics of the book of Acts, like that of Luke's Gospel, is the universality of God's plan for man's salvation. It shows the fulfillment of the plan of God begun with the election of Abraham, father of the Chosen People, through whom the blessings promised would be given to the whole world. This is now fulfilled through Christ and the Church, the New People of God.

Read Isaiah 2:1-5.

In our life

The Acts of the Apostles begins at Jerusalem. They never finish. "You shall be witnesses unto me to the ends of the earth." The verses 30-31 of ch. 28 are not a conclusion. They continue today. And **you** and **I** as members of the Church, the New People of God—of whom are we witnesses?

Points to think about

1. The spoken Gospel was the Gospel before the written Gospels: when the Church began her mission, possibly nothing of our New Testament had yet been written down. The first announcement of the Gospel was the preaching of the apostles. Only later, and little by little, was it committed to writing in the Epistles and the written Gospels. Our New Testament thus grew out of the preaching of the apostles.

2. Some of the earliest examples of this spoken Gospel are found in the sermons of the Acts of the Apostles. In fact, a careful study of these sermons reveals a remarkable similarity of themes: the preacher underlines the fulfillment of the prophetic message of the Old Testament in Jesus, His life, preaching, death and resurrection, and the giving of the Holy Spirit. The listeners are then called upon to repent in order to receive forgiveness and the gift of the Holy Spirit and new life in Christ. (These basic outlines would later form the foundation of the written Gospels and the whole of the New Testament.) Examine in this light, the sermons of Peter and Paul e.g., Acts 2:14-40, 3:12-26, 10:34-43, 13:16-41.

3. There are 18 speeches in the Acts (about 1/4 of the book).

    1:15f; 2:14f; 3:12f; 4:8f: Peter

    13:16f; 14:15f; 17:22f; 20:18f; 24:10f; 26:2f; 28:17f: Paul

    Ch. 15: Peter and James; 5:34f: Gamaliel; 7:2f: Stephen; 19:35f: the clerk of Ephesus; 24:2f: Tertullus.

4. Note how the Acts give us a good part of the life of Paul. A careful reading of it should help one to understand how, why and on what occasion certain epistles were written. In fact, the Acts furnish us with a useful link between the Gospels and the Epistles.

5. Note also the life situations or threefold milieu in which the Gospels took shape:

    (1) The prayer of the Church (liturgical milieu)

    (2) The instruction of new converts or the re-reading of Scripture to understand God's plan of salvation in Christ (catechetics)

    (3) The missionary effort: at first restricted to Palestine, but soon to extend to Asia, Europe and the ends of the world.

6. Reading the Acts helps us better to live as witnesses of the Risen Christ by our words and by our lives as the apostles did: each time Luke speaks of the Holy Spirit (e.g., 1:2, 1:8, 2:3, etc.), we are reminded it is the same Spirit who "encourages us from within." Every time we read of "conversion" (3:19, 8:2, etc.), we see it is the Lord who changes hearts. The numerous difficulties faced by the apostles and early Christians (8:1, 9:25, 12:4, etc.), widen our horizons too—"unto the ends of the earth."

7. This second volume of Luke seems to end abruptly. Perhaps Luke felt that since Paul had brought Christianity to Rome, he could bring his book to an end. The Acts of the Apostles had reached the heart of the empire.

8. The Church in her liturgy prays that all Christians may witness to the Gospel by their lives (cf. Mass for the Propagation of the Faith). May this prayer be fulfilled in us.

Selections

2:14-41	Peter's sermon at Pentecost: the birth of the Church
4:1-12	Peter's speech before the Sanhedrin
10:34-48	Cornelius' Baptism
13:13-41	Paul at Antioch

Prayer: Recite Psalm 96.
"Declare his glory among the nations."

Song: All you nations. Lucien Deiss. (PMB - 142)

Thought for the day: As a witness to his resurrection (1:22).

MY FAVORITE PASSAGES FROM THE GOSPELS
AND ACTS:

Quiz on the Gospels and Acts

1. What is the Gospel referred to in Acts 1:1?
2. Which is the shortest of the Gospels?
3. Are the Gospels of Matthew, Luke, and John known as the synoptic Gospels?
4. Which Gospel is known as the Gospel of mercy, of joy in the Holy Spirit?
5. Which evangelist often speaks of the struggle between light and darkness?
6. Which Gospel is known as the Gospel of the Church?
7. Which evangelist alone records the parable of the good Samaritan?
8. Is the idea of the "messianic secret" emphasized by Matthew or Mark?
9. Who has all 8 beatitudes, Matthew or Luke?
10. Name a miracle narrated by all 4 evangelists.

Answers on page 276.

New Testament Period at a Glance

67 B.C.   Pompeii enters Jerusalem (Judaea be-
           comes part of Roman Empire)
           c. 6 B.C. Birth of Jesus in Bethlehem

4 B.C.   Death of Herod the Great (Mt. 2:19)

14 A.D.   Accession of Tiberius Caesar (Lk. 3:1)
           c. 28 Public life of Christ

26-36 A.D. Pontius Pilate (Governor of Judaea)
           (Lk. 3:1)
                   c. 30 Death and Resurrection of
                   Christ
                   c. 36 Conversion of Paul
                   c. 47 First journey of Paul
                   c. 49 Council of Jerusalem
                   c. 60 Paul arrives in Rome

64-68 A.D. Nero's Persecution
                   c. 67 Martyrdom of Peter
                   and Paul in Rome

70 A.D.   Capture and destruction of
                   Jerusalem and temple by Titus

c. 90 A.D. Persecution under Domitian

           Death of John
100 A.D.

135 A.D.   Jews expelled from Jerusalem
           (Bar Kochba revolt)
           Complete destruction of Jerusalem
           City rebuilt by Hadrian as Aelia Capitolina

223

The Pauline Epistles

"For me, to live is Christ"
(Philippians 1:21).

"To me, though I am the very least
of all the saints, this grace was given,
to preach to the Gentiles
the unsearchable riches of Christ,
and to make all men see what is the plan
of the mystery hidden for ages in God
who created all things" (Ep. 3:8, 9).

Calendar of the life of Paul
with the Pauline epistles

(All dates are approximate)

A.D.	EPISTLES	
5-15		Born at Tarsus
30		(Death and resurrection of Jesus)
34-36		Conversion on the road to Damascus
		3 years in Arabia, Tarsus, then Antioch in Syria
		Visit to Jerusalem. Then Antioch in Syria.
47-49		I. THE FIRST MISSIONARY JOURNEY (Ac. 13 and 14)
	Galatians (according to the South Galatian Theory)	Antioch in Syria — Cyprus — Perga in Pamphylia — Lystra — Iconium — Lystra — Derbe — Lystra — Iconium — Antioch of Pisidia — Visit to Jerusalem
49		COUNCIL OF JERUSALEM (Ac. 15)
50-52		II. THE SECOND MISSIONARY JOURNEY (Ac. 15:36f.; 16; 17)
	1 and 2 Th. (from Corinth)	Antioch in Syria — Derbe — Lystra — Iconium — Antioch of Pisidia — Troas — Philippi — Thessalonica — Beroea — Athens — Corinth (1 1/2 years) — Cenchreae — Ephesus — Caesarea — Jerusalem — Antioch in Syria
53-58		III. THE THIRD MISSIONARY JOURNEY (Ac. 18:22f.)
(c. 54)	1 Co. (from Ephesus)	Antioch in Syria — Galatia and Phrygia (Derbe, Lystra, Iconium, Antioch of Pisidia) —
(c. 57)	2 Co. (from Macedonia)	Ephesus (2 yrs. and 3 months, c. 54-57) — Macedonia (Philippi, Thessalonica, Beroea)— Greece or Achaia (Athens and Corinth)

225

A.D.	EPISTLES	
		— Macedonia — Troas — Miletus — Tyre — Caesarea — Jerusalem (Jewish plot to kill Paul) —
57-58	Romans (from Corinth)	Caesarea (in prison)
60-61		IV. THE JOURNEY TO ROME (Fall to spring) Caesarea — Crete — Melita (Malta) —
61-63	Ep. — Col., Ph. — Phm. (from Rome) 1 Tm. Tt.	ROME (2 yrs. — house arrest — trial before Nero) Release from imprisonment — further traveling
64-67	Timothy	Imprisonment and martyrdom

Epistles of Paul at a Glance

EPISTLE	THEME	ADDRESSED TO	APPROXIMATE DATE	PROBABLE PLACE OF WRITING
Ga.	Q. Must one first become a Jew before becoming a Christian? A. No!	Christians in "Galatia"	48-54 (Scholars disagree)	Antioch in Syria or Ephesus
1 Th.	Exhortation to progress. Expectancy of the Parousia	Christians in Thessalonica	50-52 (2nd missionary journey)	Corinth
2 Th.	The Second Coming is yet a long way off.	,,	,,	,,
1 Co.	Problems of the local Church of Corinth in the first century (beliefs, morals, manners).	Christians in Corinth	54, during 3rd missionary journey	Ephesus
2 Co.	Personal apology. Collection for the Church in Jerusalem	,,	55-57 during 3rd missionary journey	Macedonia
Rm.	The relationship between Judaism and Christianity (The meaning of the Gospel)	Christians in Rome	57-58 3rd journey	Corinth
Ph.	Personal sentiments 1. the joy of suffering for Christ 2. thanks for the gift while in prison	Christians at Philippi	61-63 (according to some, earlier)	Rome (From Ephesus)
Col.	The primacy and pre-eminence of Christ against specific Gnostic errors	Christians at Colossae	61-63 (House arrest in Rome)	Rome
Ep.	The mystery of Christ and the Church in God's eternal plan	Christians around Ephesus or in general	61-63	,,
Phm.	Plea for Onesimus, a runaway slave, now a Christian	Philemon of the Church at Colossae	61-63	,,
1 Tm.	The organization and administration of local Churches	Timothy in Ephesus	63 or 64	Macedonia or Spain
1 Tt.	,,	Titus in Crete	63 or 64	,,
2 Tm.	Last admonitions and encouragement to "carry on" the work	Timothy in Ephesus	65-67	Rome

THE EPISTLE OF PAUL
TO THE ROMANS

The meaning
of Christianity

"The Gospel: it is the power of God for salvation to everyone who has faith" (1:16).

It is about the year 57-58 A.D. Paul is at Corinth, preparing to go to Jerusalem and from there to proceed to Rome to visit the Christian community there, on his way to Spain (cf. Rm. 15:24). He thought that his best introduction to this community would be a fairly thorough exposition of his thought on the Gospel of Christ, particularly in its relation to Judaism. The latter topic had been the subject of controversy in the early Church. With this in mind, he drew up for them a leisurely and well-thought-out statement of the meaning of Christianity as he saw it and of its relationship to the Mosaic law. The result was this longest of the Pauline letters: the epistle to the Romans.

1:1-15	Introduction
1:16—3:20	Both Jew and Gentile alike are incapable of attaining righteousness by themselves.
3:21—4:25	Hence God showed forth His "righteousness" in Christ.
5:1-21	This is gratuitously given to us in Christ.
6:1-23	This liberates us from sin
7:1-25	And from the Law
8:1-39	Because the true righteousness is life in the Spirit.
9:1—11:36	Although rejected by the Jews, God's mercy is still open to them.
12:1—15:13	What it means to be a Christian
15:14—16:27	Conclusion

In this epistle, more explicitly than in any other, Paul sets forth the powerlessness of man to liberate himself from his sinful condition and the fullness of the redeeming grace of God in Christ through the Holy Spirit.

In the
Old Testament

The great prophets of the Old Testament foresaw that a characteristic of the messianic age would be an extraordinary outpouring of the Spirit. This would make possible the inward renewal indispensable for a faithful observance of the law of God.

Compare Rm. 1:16—3:20 with Jr. 9:24-26 and 31:31-34.

"For all these nations and all the house of Israel are uncircumcised at heart" (Jr. 9:26).

"The real circumcision is a matter of the heart, spiritual and not literal" (Rm. 2:29).

In the present salvific moment

A Christian is never altogether made. Paradoxically, he has always to become that which he is. It is not enough to **know** that we are living by Christ. One has to live and **be** it. "Do not model yourselves on the behavior of the world around you, but let your behavior change, modeled by your new mind. This is the only way to discover the will of God and know what is good, what it is that God wants, what is the perfect thing to do" (Rm. 12:2) (JB).

Points to think about

1. Some of the key words of this epistle, such as Gospel, justice of God, faith, etc., touch upon some of the fundamental themes of Paul's theology. Highlight them as you read. They have been a source of inspiration to theologians through the centuries.

2. Note how 1:3-6 briefly summarizes the message of the epistle.

3. Note how for St. Paul faith, which is one of the central themes of the epistle, is a response of the whole human being's call in Christ. It is not only intellectual assent but trust and obedience; it is reliance on God and not on self; it is a faith that expresses itself in love (Rm. 1:5, 3:3f., 6:17, 10:16, 16:26, etc.).

4. Note also the tremendous importance of the Holy Spirit in the Christian life. When we are received into Christ by faith and Baptism, the Holy Spirit dwells in us, makes us sons of God, and becomes the principle of a new life in Christ. When Christ is present, there is unity and equality in diversity (3:26-29). Is Christ present in the world of today?

Selections

1:16, 17; 3:21-26	The power of God saving all through faith in Christ
5:1-11; 6:1-11	Looking forward to God's glory "the love of God has been poured through the Holy Spirit into our hearts."
8:12-17	"Everyone moved by the Spirit is a son of God."
11:33-36	How wonderful is God's wisdom?

Prayer: Recite Psalm 117.
       Praise the Lord, all nations.
       God of unchanging power and light, bring lasting salvation, we pray, to all mankind through Him who is the Savior, Jesus Christ, Your Son, our Lord. Amen (cf. Rm. 3:21-26).

Song: Amazing Grace. Traditional Negro spiritual.

Thought for the day: "I am not ashamed of the Gospel, it is the power of God for salvation to everyone who has faith..." (1:16).

CORINTHIANS

The standards
of the kingdom

"For no other foundation can anyone lay than that which is laid, which is Jesus Christ" (1 Co. 3:11).

In the world of Paul, Corinth was one of the most important political and commercial centers of the time, and was notorious for every kind of vice. St. Paul's letters to the Corinthians show how difficult it must have been to live as a Christian in the midst of such a pagan environment.

Now open your Bible and read:

The first epistle of St. Paul to the Corinthians.

1:1-9   Introduction

1:10—6:20 Abuses at Corinth
           Factions: 1:10—4:21
           Scandals: 5:1—6:20

7:1—15:58 Answers to questions
           about marriage and celibacy: 7:1-40
           about eating food offered to idols: 8:1—11:1
           about (order in) Christian worship: 11:2-34
           about the use of charismata: 12:1—14:40
           about the resurrection of the dead: 15:1-58

16:1-12   Personal matters
16:13-24   Conclusion

The letters of Paul and of the other apostles were written, for the most part, to meet the daily concerns of the early Church, and dealt with the day-to-day problems occasioned by the practice of the Christian Faith at that time. Yet, the message of this letter, like that of the rest

231

of the letters, is as actual for us today as for the Christians of the first century, for Paul hardly ever solves a particular problem without referring to the most basic and enduring principles of the Christian Faith.

In the Old Testament

In chapter 10 of this letter, Paul compares the life of the Church to the march of the wandering people of God in the desert. The whole people received the promise, yet some fell away due to unfaithfulness. He warns the Christians who form part of the New People of God enjoying still more marvelous favors and promises that they could show themselves unworthy too.

Read the book of Numbers (14:20-35).

In our life

We sometimes tend to think that of all periods of history, our times are the worst. These letters show us that human nature changes very little and problems similar to those we have in the Church today already existed at other times too. "Be awake to all dangers; stay firm in faith; be brave and be strong" (1 Co. 16:13) (JB).

	The 2nd epistle to the Corinthians
1:1-11	Introduction
1:12—7:16	The clearing up of past misunderstanding and justification of his actions
8:1—9:15	Concerning the collection for the Church of Jerusalem
10:1—13:10	Paul's personal apologia
13:11-13	Conclusion

Points to think about

1. A careful reading of these two epistles suggests that Paul actually wrote, not two but four letters to the

Corinthians. Two of these letters are lost, or, as some modern critics suspect, have been incorporated into the two letters we have in the Bible (cf. 1 Co. 5:9). Do you think that the 2nd letter to the Corinthians could be divided into two letters: chs. 1-9 and chs. 10-13?

2. To understand the full import of these letters, one has to go back in mind to the time of Paul, when Corinth was a city of 600,000 persons, of whom 400,000 were slaves. Besides being a port of international trade, it was famous as a center of education and culture, and for its universities, its games, its temple of Aphrodite with some thousand prostitutes. In this city of a minority of free men living in luxury amid a majority of slaves, Paul founded the Church of Corinth. He trusted in the presence of the living Christ and the power of His Holy Spirit to overcome all difficulties.

3. Were the adversaries of Paul mentioned in the second Epistle to the Corinthians: Palestinian Jews or Gentiles? They cannot be identified with certainty.

4. It is when we have to live through serious difficulties that we are obliged to say clearly what we are and what we want. Paul does this in his letters. He goes to the bottom of things and explains the meaning of his life and apostolate (cf. 2 Co. 1:12—2:13). Only one thing matters for Paul. What he believes is also what he lives. That's Paul. The best way to come to know Paul is to read his own words, and re-read them again and again. They speak for themselves, better than any commentary can. See, for instance, 1 Co. 5:7, 8, the beautiful words by which Paul teaches that the Christian is united with the sacrificed and risen Christ in an unending Passover.

Selections

1 Co. 2:1-9	Paul's preaching: not human philosophy
1 Co. 7:1-40	Virginity and marriage
1 Co. 11:23-27	The Lord's supper

| 1 Co. 13:1-13 | The greatest thing in the world: Love |
| 2 Co. 11:16—12:10 | The great apologia |

Prayer: Teach us, O Lord, that it is in self-giving that we find our true self, that it is in forgiving that we are forgiven, that it is in thanksgiving that we experience Your grace, that it is in dying, that we are raised to life. Amen. (Prayer of St. Francis of Assisi)

Song: Awake and live, O you who sleep. Lucien Deiss. (BHP II 70)

Thought for the day: "Cleanse out the old leaven that you may be a new lump, as you really are unleavened. For Christ, our paschal lamb has been sacrificed" (1 Co. 5:7).

GALATIANS

"When Christ freed us, he meant us to remain free" (5:1) (JB).

The Jewish Christians of some of the churches Paul had founded on his first missionary journey were being persuaded by some to insist that Gentile converts be compelled to be circumcised and observe the Mosaic law. These "Judaizers," in order to attain their end more effectively, were seeking to throw doubt on Paul's own authority and his teaching.

Now open your Bible and read:

The epistle of Paul to the Galatians.

1:1-10	Introduction
1:11—2:21	Paul's defense of his apostolic authority; although approved by the other apostles, his mission is from Christ Himself.
3:1—4:31	It is faith that justifies, not the law, from which faith sets us free.
5:1—6:10	Various exhortations
6:11-18	Conclusion

As this is, perhaps, one of the earliest documents of the New Testament to be written down, it is interesting to note that, for the primitive Church, the Gospel of Christ has something unique about it and had a very definite meaning. This is reflected in Paul's teaching of the fact of Christ's resurrection, and the consequences of it for the Christian. Later, Paul would explain its implications more fully in his epistle to the Romans.

In the
Old Testament

Our call as Christians goes back to the call of Abraham, not through the observance of the meticulous prescriptions of the letter of the Mosaic law, but through

faith in Christ. "If you are Christ's, then you are Abraham's offspring, heirs according to the promise" (3:29).
Read Gn. 22:15-19 (highlight v. 18).

In the present salvific moment

Reflecting on what St. Paul says about the tension that exists in us between the spirit and the desires of the flesh (Ga. 5:16-26), we should ask for the grace to live by the Spirit so that we may have joy and peace. The fundamental proof of Paul's gospel of grace and freedom was the Christian experience of new life in Christ, a new life which blossoms in "love, joy and peace" (5:22).

Points to think about

1. Note Paul's allegorical equation summarizing his thought so impressively and concisely. Hagar=slave-woman = Sinai = law = flesh = earthly Jerusalem = slavery and slaves. Sarah = freewoman = promise = faith = Spirit = heavenly Jerusalem = mother of freedom and free men, (cf. Ga. 4:21-26). 5:13-26 emphasizes the practical conclusion of his teaching by emphasizing the right conception and use of this freedom.

2.   "O foolish Galatians!" (3:1) Who are these Galatians? There are two principal opinions. They could be the communities mentioned in Acts: Antioch of Pisidia, Derbe, Lystra, Iconium (South Galatian theory), or they could refer to the communities of Galatia proper, i.e., of the original central kingdom of central Anatolia (North Galatian theory) in Asia Minor (modern Turkey).

3. The dogmatic content of the letter is more fully developed in the epistle to the Romans. But this letter to the Galatians is invaluable for the pages of Pauline autobiography it furnishes us. Note it carefully (1:11—2:21).

4. Paul epitomizes his teaching in a unique phrase "in Christ." It is used 164 times in Paul's letters.

Selections

Prayer: Recite Psalm 98.

"All the ends of the earth have seen...."

Almighty God, grant us the true circumcision of the Spirit, that our hearts and all our members, being mortified from all worldly and carnal lusts, we may in all things obey Your blessed will through Jesus Christ our Lord (The Book of Common Prayer).

Song: In Christ, there is no East or West. Ray Repp. (BCW - 19)

Thought for the day: "It does not matter whether a person is circumcised or not; what matters is for him to become an altogether new creature" (Ga. 6:15) (JB).

EPHESIANS, PHILIPPIANS, COLOSSIANS

Paul writes from prison

EPHESIANS

The heart
of the mystery

"Before the world was made, he chose us...in Christ" (1:4) (JB).

The epistle to the Ephesians is also concerned, like the epistle to the Colossians, with the mystery of Christ. But here the Apostle enlarges his vision to reveal the secret of the call of all nations to form the Church, the Mystical Body of Christ.

1:1-2	Address	
1:3—3:21	Exposition of the mystery of salvation	
	1:15—2:10	Prayer that they may perceive more profoundly this mystery
	2:11-22	The unity of Jews and Gentiles in Christ
	3:1-21	The proclamation of the mystery to the Gentiles
4:1—6:20	The exigencies of a Christian life	
	4:1-16	Unity and diversity in the same spirit
	4:17-24	The new man created for holiness
	4:25—5:2	Love
	5:3-20	The darkness of sin and the light of the Spirit
	5:21—6:9	Christian family life
	6:10-20	The Christian and the spiritual combat
	6:21-24	Conclusion

This epistle is particularly striking for its loftiness of thought. In it, the Apostle tries to communicate to his readers, as far as human words permit, the knowledge he has received by special illumination of the Holy Spirit of the "mystery of Christ" and of God's magnificent plan of salvation in Christ for all men of all ages.

In the
Old Testament

In this epistle, St. Paul takes an overall view, as it were, of salvation history as revealed in the Old Testament and in the Bible as a whole. The mystery of Christ is already present in the call of Abraham, in the revelation at Sinai and in the Davidic covenant.

Read Gn. 22:15-18; Ex. 19:1-8; 2 S. 7:4-17.

In our life

It is only by prayer and faith that one can enter into the mystery of God's plan. Every time we take up the Bible to read, we should ask humbly that we too may be given the grace "to comprehend," with all the saints, what is the breadth and the length, the height and the depth, until knowing the love of Christ, which is beyond all knowledge we are filled with the fullness of God (cf. Ep. 3:18-19) (JB).

Selections

1:3-10 The mystery of God's plan
3:7-13 The unsearchable riches of Christ
5:1-14 Walk in love as Christ loved us.

Prayer: Recite 3:14-21, uniting yourself with the prayer Paul made for you.

O God, make us hear the call to be Christian. To be—to be human—to be Christian! To be free, joyful, peaceful, forgiving! May this be our missionary presence today, here, now and every day of our lives, through Christ our Lord. Amen.

Song: There is one Lord. Lucien Deiss. (PMB - 168)

Thought for the day: "To know the love of Christ which surpasses all knowledge" (3:19).

PHILIPPIANS

Tenderly in the heart
of Christ (1:18-19)

"...that I may know him and the power of his resurrection" (3:10).

Philippi was also one of the important cities of Macedonia at the time of Paul. It was Paul's first contact with Europe. He seems to have always had a special affection for the Church he founded there. In this epistle, he shares with them the joy of suffering for Christ.

1:1-2	Address
1:3-11	Thanks and prayer
1:12-26	My chains.... Life to me is Christ.
1:27—2:18	Christian life: have the same mind as Christ.
2:19—3:1	The mission of Timothy and Epaphroditus
3:2—4:1	The prize to which God calls us
4:2-20	The final advice and thanks
4:21-23	Conclusion

Unlike in Colossians and Ephesians, there is no elaborate theological development in this letter (except for the unique passages of 2:6-11). It seems to have been written simply to share with them what he was living. Paul is in prison for the sake of the Gospel. It is there that he discovers true joy.

In the
Old Testament

Paul, in the midst of his sufferings, and contemplating the death and resurrection of Christ, thinks of the contrast between the first Adam of Genesis (chs. 2 and 3), and Christ, the New Adam. The first Adam, although he was a man, sinned by wanting to "be like God" (Gn. 3:5). Christ, on the contrary, although He was the

Son of God, humbled Himself to our condition and became obedient unto death.

Read Isaiah ch. 53.

In our life

The Church sees in Ph. 2:5-11 the inner meaning and value of the events of Christ's passion, and uses this message of the epistle as the dominant theme of the last three days of Holy Week.

Selections

1:19-26   For me to live is Christ.
2:5-11   The mind of Christ
3:7-14   For His sake, I have suffered the loss of all things.

Prayer:

"Soul of Christ, sanctify me;
Body of Christ, save me;
Blood of Christ, inebriate me;
Water from the side of Christ, wash me;
Passion of Christ, strengthen me;
O good Jesus, hear me;
Within Your wounds, hide me;
And do not permit me to be separated from You;
From the Evil Force, defend me;
At the hour of death, call me;
And bid me come to You,
That with Your saints, I may praise You,
Forever and ever. Amen."
(Favorite prayer of Ignatius of Loyola)

Song: Into your hands. Ray Repp. (HYC - II-20)

Thought for the day: "I press on toward the goal...the upward call of God in Christ Jesus" (3:14).

COLOSSIANS

Through him and for him (1:15-18)

The writing of this epistle was possibly occasioned by the need to clarify certain problems that had arisen in the Church at Colossae about the primacy and pre-eminence of Christ. An early heresy, probably inspired by Gnostic ideas, seems to have tried to place Christ below the angels and below certain cosmic powers. In answer to this, the Apostle wrote this letter.

1:1-14	Introduction
1:15—2:7	The person and the work of Christ: His primacy
2:8-23	Warning against the errors propagated at Colossae: the all-sufficiency of Christ
3:1—4:6	Various recommendations: new life in Christ
4:7-18	Conclusion

The central theme of the epistle is the pre-eminence of Christ in the universe. In Him is the fullness of God. He is not only the head of the Church, whose members form His Mystical Body, but also of creation. In Christ, the great unity of the divine plan, which embraces all creation, is revealed.

In the Old Testament

St. Paul's language about the pre-existence of Christ is reminiscent of the passages in the Wisdom books of the Old Testament which personify the Wisdom of God.

Read Proverbs 8:22-31; Sirach 24:3-14; Wisdom 7:22-27.

In the present salvific moment

Through Baptism, the Christian participates in the death and resurrection of Christ and as a member of His Mystical Body, he is called to live a heavenly life "hid with Christ in God" to "appear with him in glory" when He comes again (cf. Col. 3:1-4).

Selections

Colossians: 1:15-20 The image of the unseen God
3:1-17   Life in Christ

Prayer: Heavenly Father, since we have been raised with Christ in our Baptism, may we seek the things that are above, where Christ is seated at Your right hand. May we be intent on the things that are above, not on things that are on earth. We ask this through the same Christ, Your Son, our Lord. Amen. (cf. Col. 3:1, 2).

Song: You alone are holy. Lucien Deiss. (BHP - II 72)

Thought for the day: "You must live your whole life according to the Christ you have received—Jesus the Lord" (Col. 2:6) (JB).

Points to think about on the "three epistles of the captivity"

1. These three epistles, so-called letters of captivity, present a positive exposition of Christianity. In fact, the epistle to the Ephesians is one of the most doctrinal of all the Pauline letters. The "Gospel" is the "good news" about the "mystery," the mystery of the divine plan of salvation. Christian life is an entering into this mystery. The Church is the mysterious (mystical) Body of Christ, in which Jew and Gentile become one in Christ.

2. Many passages in these epistles can be converted into prayer, e.g., Col. 2:6-7; 3:1-4; Ph. 3:8-14; Ep. 1:17-19; 3:16-19.

3. In a manner more significant than other epistles, these show how before preaching Christ, Paul lives Christ. See, for example, Col. 1:24—2:5.

4. The great lesson of these epistles of the captivity is that a religious life, without Christ, even if it be full of activity, makes no sense. See Ph. 3:8-10; Col. 2:6-23; Ep. 2:10.

5. Note the unique Christological hymn in Ph. 2:6-11. Its six verses are a wonderful summary of the Gospel message as a whole: (1) the divine pre-existence of Christ; (2) the "humiliation" of the incarnation; (3) the abasement of the cross; (4) the exaltation of the Christ; (5) the homage of the universe; (6) the glorious name given to the exalted Christ.

6. In your reading of the epistle to the Ephesians, highlight the places where the plan of God and its consequences for us are underscored, e.g. Ep. 1:4, 9; 2:7; 3:4, 9. In the epistle to the Philippians, highlight the places where "joy" is spoken of, e.g., 1:18, 25; 2:17-18, 28-29; 3:1; 4:10, etc. In Colossians, where Paul emphasizes the new life in the risen Christ, e.g., 3:1-4, 5, 9-10, 12-15.

7. Note the Christological hymn in Col. 1:15-20. Can you decipher how the author draws on concepts and terminology found in the wisdom literature of the Old Testament to describe the central role of Christ?

8. Once again, do not lose sight of the general message of the epistles to the Ephesians and Colossians for today: God wills that the human race, which stands in great part alienated from God and is consequently fragmented, with all the frightful results of that state (two great World Wars and the contemporary situation), should be reconciled to its Creator in Christ and find freedom in this life in Christ. The mission of the Church and our mission as Christians is to work for this reconciliation. First of all, Christians, as members of the community of salvation, must manifest this unity among themselves, as an example to the world, "that all may be one" (Jn. 17:21).

I AND II THESSALONIANS

Christian life is an intense expectation, a living hope

"...to lead a life worthy of God, who calls you into his kingdom of glory" (1 Th. 2:12).

The two epistles to the Thessalonians were probably addressed from Corinth to the Christians of Thessalonica in the course of the Apostle's second missionary voyage about the year 50-52 A.D. In them, the Apostle encourages them to live up to the new Christian life they have received and solves some of their difficulties. Among other things Paul answers their anxious question about the lot of their dead and the second coming of the Lord.

The first epistle to the Thessalonians

Chs. 1-2	Paul reminds them of the selflessness with which he preached the Gospel to them.
Ch. 3	Paul's joy at their faith and fidelity
4:1-12	Exhortation to continue faithful
4:13-18	The second coming of the Lord and the lot of the dead
Ch. 5	Final exhortations

The second epistle to the Thessalonians

Ch. 1	The Apostle's joy in their faith
2:1-12	Parousia of the Lord, not imminent
2:13—3:18	Encouragement and closing appeal to fidelity

These two letters are considered by many to be the first letters of Paul, in fact, the first written pages of the New Testament. Already he brings us straight to the point. What is Christian life? It is entering willingly into God's plan of salvation. It is a march forward in faith. It is an intense expectation, a living hope (1 Th. 3:11-13).

These letters introduce us to the heart of the great Apostle, his selfless zeal and dedication to his calling.

In the
Old Testament

In the Old Testament, we see the hope of the kingdom of God, which was to be realized in the advent of the Messiah, become clearer with the development of revelation. The synoptic Gospels are also dominated by the expectation of this kingdom of God, but Paul expressly deals at length with the implications of this Christian hope.

In our life

Christian life is a life of hope and expectation. This expectation is based not on our successes and our failures but on God's power to realize His plan for us in Christ.

Points to think about

1. The Thessalonica of these two letters is the Saloniki of today. Because of its harbor and its situation on the route from Asia to Rome (the Ignatian way), it had become a thriving city in the time of Paul. It was the capital of Macedonia for a couple of centuries.

2. Note and highlight as you read these epistles the lines where Paul explains the basic features of Christian life.

3. How different life has become for so many who are Christians only in name, living as if there were no tomorrow to look forward to: "Eat, drink and make merry, for tomorrow we die."

Selections

I Thessalonians
  1:4-10 Christian life: an expectation (v. 10)
  4:3-8   Called by God to be holy
II Thessalonians
  2:1-12 Do not get excited too soon: the Second
          coming is yet a long way off.

Prayer: Grant us today, O Lord, the seeing eye, the hearing ear, the understanding mind, the loving heart, so that we may see Your glory, hear Your Word, understand Your truth and answer to Your love. Amen.

Song: Without seeing You, we love You. Lucien Deiss. (BHP - II 63)

Thought for the day: May the God of peace make us perfect and holy (cf. 1 Th. 5:23) (JB).

THE PASTORAL EPISTLES
TO TIMOTHY AND TITUS

In the Church of the living God (1 Tm. 3:15)

The two epistles to Timothy and one to Titus are called pastoral epistles because their main theme is instruction regarding the organization and administration of the local Churches. Timothy, a native of Lystra in Lycaonia, was Paul's disciple and traveling companion, and later became the bishop of Ephesus. Titus was another Greek collaborator of Paul. The contents and instructions of the first epistle to Timothy and the epistle to Titus are similar and written possibly from Macedonia or Spain. In the second epistle to Timothy, however, the Apostle, in prison and approaching his martyrdom, gives his disciple his last admonitions.

1st epistle to Timothy:

1:1-2	Address of greeting
1:3-20	Combat against the false teachers
2:1—6:2	Certain disciplinary matters in worship and in the ministry
6:3-10	Teaching and practice of false teachers
6:11-19	Advice to Timothy regarding good life and example
6:20-21	Conclusion

The epistle to Titus:

1:1-4	Address and greetings
1:5-16	Duties of Titus as a bishop and against false teachers
2:1—3:11	Some disciplinary matters (similar to those in 1 Tm.)
3:12-15	Conclusion

2nd epistle to Timothy:

1:1-2	Address
1:3—2:13	Exhortation to fidelity after Paul's example and to carry on the work

These epistles are valuable not only for the picture they present of the difficulties and problems of the early Church, but also and particularly because of the Apostle's pastoral directives regarding ministers and the government of the Church. They were highly valued by the apostolic Fathers and can serve as a handbook for ministers of the Church, and all who work with them.

In the
Old Testament

The admonitions of the Apostle remind us of some of the hard things the prophets of the Old Testament had to say about the spiritual shepherds of the people who neglected their duties.

Read the book of Ezekiel 34:1-31.

In our life

The reading of these epistles brings home to us in a forceful manner the qualities needed in ministers of the Church and the serious responsibility they are called upon to shoulder. Let us pray for the Church that she may always be blessed with worthy ministers.

Points to think about

1. Highlight and reflect on the texts that sum up the essentials of the Christian life, e.g., 1 Tm. 1:12-17; Tt. 1:1-4; 2:11-14; 2 Tm. 1:6-10; 2:8-13.

2. Note also the qualities which Paul thinks a minister of the Church should have: 1 Tm. 3:4-10; 4:8-16; Tt. 2:1; 3:8; 2 Tm. 1:6-9; 2:22-26; 3:14-17, and the advice he gives to different categories of Christians: the rich (1 Tm. 6:17-19), the older men (Tt. 2:1), the older women (Tt. 2:3), younger women (Tt. 2:5), younger men (Tt. 2:7), slaves (1 Tm. 6:1-2, Tt. 2:9).

3. Note the emphasis on saving grace and Christian behavior in 2:11-15.

Selections

1 Tm. 3:14—4:16	In the Church of the living God
Tt. 2:1-15	Teaching in accordance with sound doctrine
2 Tm. 2:1-13	Be God's good soldier.
2 Tm. 4:1-8	Paul's farewell charge to his disciple

Prayer:

Lord, teach me to be generous;
To serve You as You deserve;
To give and not to count the cost;
To fight and not to heed the wounds;
To toil and not to seek for rest;
To labor and not to look for any reward,
Save to know that I do Your holy will. Amen.
(Prayer of St. Ignatius of Loyola)

Song: Keep in mind. Lucien Deiss. (BHP - I 2)

Thought for the day: "Remember Jesus Christ, risen from the dead...if we have died with him, we shall also live with him" (2 Tm. 2:8,11).

EPISTLE TO PHILEMON

Slave
and brother

"If you consider me your partner, receive him as you would receive me" (v. 17).

This epistle is Paul's letter to a Christian named Philemon in the church at Colossae. Paul pleads for one of Philemon's runaway slaves, Onesimus, whom Paul had met in Rome and had converted to Christianity. Receive him as a brother Christian is Paul's request.

1-7 Salutation
8-21 Plea for Onesimus
22-25 Personal greeting

Although this epistle is only a short twenty verses, it places before us in concise terms the Pauline doctrine of the dignity of the Christian and of the love that Christians should have for one another by reason of their union in Christ.

In our life

Note how St. Paul does not expressly condemn the social institution of slavery which existed in his time. But he solves the problem by applying Christian principles to the relations that should exist between master and slave. Perhaps we have something to learn from this way of acting of the Apostle when we treat of problems which pertain also to the temporal sphere.

Prayer: Recite Psalm 130 for all who suffer oppression and misery in the world.

Song: Come away to the land of freedom. Ray Repp. (HYC - II - 88)

Thought for the day: "No longer as a slave but...as a beloved brother" (v. 16).

251

THE EPISTLE TO THE HEBREWS

"A new covenant...an eternal inheritance" (9:15).

The epistle to the Hebrews has been considered somewhat apart from the other epistles attributed to Paul because of its peculiar style and manner of presentation. It is a beautiful comparison of the Old and New Testaments.

1. 1:1—10:18   Christ, the Son, brings a New Covenant to be accepted in faith and trust.

    1:1-4   Christ, the Son of God

    1:5—2:18   Superior to the angels

    3:1-6   Superior to Moses

    3:7—4:11   Fidelity and perseverance

    4:12-13   The Word of God

    4:14—6:20   The priesthood of Jesus Christ higher than the levitical priesthood

    8:1—10:18   The two Covenants: the Old and the New

2. 10:19—12:29   Necessity of fidelity to this New Covenant and of advancing toward the everlasting city

3. 13:1-25   Conclusion

By means of well-founded arguments based on the Old Testament, the author of this epistle admirably demonstrated how the Gospel constitutes the full realization of what the Old Testament possessed only in image and shadow. This Gospel is actual today as the history of salvation continues in the Church, the New Israel.

In the Old Testament

The great prophets of the Old Testament foretold the coming of a new and eternal Covenant to replace the old one.

Read Jeremiah 31:31-34 and Ezekiel 36:25-28; 37:1-28.

In our life

The Church is the People of God who are on the march toward God and the heavenly sanctuary where Christ has first entered by His sacrifice. The Christian who perseveres will arrive there through Christ.

Points to think about

1. Highlight the texts that indicate the People of God as a people on the march toward God, a pilgrim people. For example: 2:1; 3:11; 4:1, 3, 16.

2. Other texts worth noting:
>   1:1-4 (a résumé of the whole epistle)
>   4:12-13 (the power of God's word)
>   5:1-10 (Jesus, compassionate high priest)
>   8:6 (the New Covenant)
>   10:32-36; 12:1-4 (the need of perseverance)

3. The comparison between what was **shadow** (8:5, 8:13), imperfect (before Christ), and that which is reality, accomplished (in Christ), runs through the whole epistle. In fact, the teaching of the epistle could be briefly seen as centered on the Paschal mystery.
>   1) The Paschal mystery prefigured in the Old Testament
>   2) The Paschal mystery fulfilled in Jesus
>   3) The Paschal mystery lived in the Church

Are **we** living the Paschal mystery?

4. Try to see how the author demonstrates the central place the Paschal mystery holds in the economy of salvation and how it should be lived in our lives.

5. How is the universal "priesthood" of the faithful emphasized in the epistle?

Selections

1:1-14	The pre-eminence of Christ
4:14—5:10	Jesus, our great and compassionate high priest
12:1-4	The importance of perseverance

Prayer: Recite Psalm 110.
"After the order of Melchisedech" (110:4).

Song: Jesus Christ, the Faithful Witness. Lucien Deiss. (BHP II 64)

Thought for the day: "Let us run with perseverance the race that is set before us, looking to Jesus, the pioneer and perfecter of our faith" (12:1-2).

MY FAVORITE PASSAGES FROM THE ACTS AND PAULINE EPISTLES:

Quiz on the "Pauline" epistles

1. Which is the longest of the Pauline epistles?

2. Name the epistle known as the "charter of Christian liberty."

3. Which epistle compares marriage to the union of Christ and the Church?

4. "If you have been raised with Christ, seek the things that are above where Christ is seated at the right hand of God."
   In which epistle are these words found?

5. Are I and II Corinthians called the "pastoral epistles"?

6. Mark correct answer: The last epistle written by Paul was probably
   a. Romans
   b. 2 Timothy

7. It was easy to live as a Christian in the Corinth of St. Paul's day. True or false?

8. "Now faith is the assurance of things hoped for, the conviction of things unseen." Is this quote from: Romans or Hebrews?

9. "If I speak in the tongues of men and of angels, but have not love, I am a noisy gong, or a clanging cymbal."
   In which epistle are these words found?

10. In which epistle does St. Paul speak of the resurrection of the dead at length?

    Answers on page 276.

JAMES

Be doers of the word and not hearers only (1:22).

The epistle of James contains, for the most part, only moral precepts. But they are valuable precepts on true devotion, justice, charity and the like. The author passes quickly from one idea to another; consequently it is difficult to make a logical division.

Now open your Bible and read:

Although it is difficult to find a logical development of the thought contained in this epistle, it is remarkable for its eminently practical character, the aptness of its illustrations, and its bold application to daily life of the spirit of the Sermon on the Mount.

In the
Old Testament

This collection of moral exhortations, the content of the epistle, are in the vein of the Wisdom literature of the Old Testament.

Read e.g., Proverbs 6:16-19.

257

In our life

Like the book of Proverbs and Sirach, this epistle is best read a little at a time. Focusing this light in this way on our lives, we can see how far we are affected by the current image of "Christians by name only."

Points to think about

1. Note the texts that stress the qualities of authentic Christian faith.

> (It is not the things that pass away that matter) 1:23-25
>
> (Concern for the poor and the general welfare) 2:2-3

2. From James, servant of God and of the Lord Jesus Christ: Greetings to the twelve tribes of the Dispersion (1:1). Who is this James? More than one person in the New Testament has this name: (1) James, brother of John, called to be an apostle (cf. Mt. 4:21, 10:2). (2) James, son of Alphaeus, another of the twelve mentioned in the list of apostles (Mt. 10:3). (3) James, the "brother of the Lord" (Mt. 13:55), head of the primitive community in Jerusalem (cf. Acts 12:17, 15:13ff.). It is this last mentioned James, to whom this Catholic epistle is generally attributed.

3. A first reading of the epistle to the Romans and this epistle might give the impression that Paul and James have different notions of "faith." But if you read them carefully, you will see that they are actually emphasizing different aspects of the same thing. Both underscore the necessity of **authentic faith** for salvation. Paul insists on authentic **faith,** while James emphasizes **authentic** faith. (The Holy Spirit is the principal author of holy Scripture and He cannot contradict Himself.)

Selections

> 1:19-27 Be doers of the word
> 3:1-12 True religion shows itself in restrained speech.

5:1-6   A warning to the rich
5:13-20 The power of prayer

Prayer: Recite Psalm 49.

Man cannot abide in his pomp, he is like the beasts that perish.

Each day passes and evening comes. Which day in our lives will never reach the evening? At that moment, Lord, let us merit to live eternally in Your light that never grows dim. (Chiara Lubich)

Song: Whatsoever you do. Rev. W. F. Jabusch. (HYC - I - 29)

Thought for the day: Whoever brings back a sinner from the error of his way will save his soul from death and will cover a multitude of sins (5:20).

FIRST EPISTLE OF PETER

A priestly
people

"You are a chosen race, a royal priesthood..." (2:9).

With the lapse of time, the Christian community became completely separated from the community of Israel. At the same time, it was entering on a period of persecution on the part of the powerful Roman empire. In these difficult circumstances, Peter addressed a letter of encouragement to Christians to strengthen and sustain their faith.

Now open your Bible and read:

The letter of Peter does not have the doctrinal development of the letters of Paul but it brings home to us a basic truth very relevant today: the universal call to sanctity of the People of God. It is a reminder to the faithful that they are all called to sanctity by reason of their baptismal consecration; to the hierarchy, bishops and priests, that they are not just set apart from the rest of the People of God, but have their place right in the bosom of the Church "to be examples to the flock"

(5:3) of authentic Christian life; to religious today that their life of consecration is, before all else, the Christian life of the baptized carried to its perfection.

In the
Old Testament

In the first section of this letter, St. Peter explains how God's plan for man's salvation, begun by God under the Old Covenant, is now fulfilled through Christ in the Church, the New People of God.

Read the book of Exodus 19:1-8 (note especially v. 6) and compare with 1 Peter 2:9.

In our life

In our prayers, we should think often of the suffering Christians in the "Church of Silence" the world over, for we are united with them in Christ, by a solidarity that transcends all boundaries.

Points to think about

1. Note and highlight the texts that:
   a. Make allusions to Baptism, which should give orientation to one's life.
   b. Show the attitude of the heart of Peter, shepherd of souls
   c. Hint of persecution
2. Other texts, such as:
   1:2-12 a great Trinitarian hymn

Exegetes think that the letter of Peter is closely linked to the primitive liturgy and particularly to that of Baptism. 1:13—2:10 has been called by some a baptismal homily (1:13-21 before Baptism and 1:22—2:10 after Baptism). Read it and see what you think of this opinion.

4. Note the striking passage on the dynamic power of the Word of God (1:22-25). Do we forget this in practice?

Selections

1:13—2:10	Authentic Christian life (highlight 1:20 and 2:9)
4:12-19	Encouragement in time of trial (highlight verse 13)

Prayer: O God, source of all grace, we pray for our suffering Christian brethren the world over, that You, who called them to eternal glory in Christ, may Yourself after they have suffered a little while, perfect, steady and strengthen and firmly establish them through the same Christ our Lord (cf. 1 P. 5:10).

Song: Priestly people, holy people. Lucien Deiss. (BHP -I 34)

Thought for the day: You are a chosen race, a royal priesthood, a holy nation, God's own people (1 P. 2:9).

THE SECOND EPISTLE OF PETER
AND THE EPISTLE OF JUDE

Beware of false
prophets (2 P. 2:1)

The second epistle of Peter and the epistle of Jude are apparently closely related to each other. Their themes and content are also remarkably similar.

Now open your Bible and read:

1. The second epistle of Peter
   - 1:1-2   Salutation
   - 1:3-21   Motivation for progress in virtue
   - 2:1-22   Warning against false teachers
   - 3:1-10   The second coming of the Lord
   - 3:11-18 Concluding doxology
2. The epistle of Jude
   - 1-4   Address and reason for the letter
   - 5-19   Description of and warning against false teachers
   - 20-25   Conclusion and doxology

The main object of both letters is the refutation of false doctrines spread by false prophets who were, in addition, leading dissolute lives. Both are an urgent exhortation to faith and love of God by reminding the faithful of the second coming of the Lord.

In the
Old Testament

The prophets of the Old Testament, too, often had to speak to the people of the "Day of the Lord," to draw them away from false prophets who misled them. Read for instance, Jr. 23:1-17.

In our life

The reminder of these two epistles "to be on our guard" is as actual and pertinent to us in our times as it was to their original readers.

Points to think about

1. Note the similarity between the two letters, e.g., 2 P. 2:1-18 and Jude 4-13.

2. Read carefully 2 P. 1:12-21. Apostolic authority in the Church

3. Reflect on the beautiful doxology in Jude 24-25.

4. In the liturgy of the season of Advent, the Church, by reminding us of the first coming of the Savior, prepares us also for the second coming of the Lord. May this liturgical season be one of true spiritual renewal for us every year.

Selections

> 2 P. 1:12-21 The apostolic witness and the Word of God
> 2 P. 3:1-10 The Day of the Lord: Christian faith and hope
> Jude vv. 3-19 False teachers

Prayer: Recite Psalm 50.
"To him who orders his way aright I will show the salvation of God."

Song: The coming of our God. A. Williams. (HYC - I - 243)

Thought for the day: To the only God, our Savior through Jesus Christ, our Lord, be glory, majesty, dominion and authority before all time, now, and forever (Jude 24, 25).

FIRST EPISTLE OF JOHN

Walk in
the Light (1:7)

Toward the end of the first century, A.D., the Church of Asia Minor seems to have been faced with a heresy. This heresy apparently took the form of an attempt on the part of some to minimize the importance of Christ as God's chosen way of revealing Himself to men and to make light of moral rectitude, especially fraternal charity. Possibly to meet this danger, the apostle wrote this letter.

Now open your Bible and read:

The first epistle of John

1:1-4	Prologue: The Incarnation
1:5—2:17	What Christianity means in practice
2:18-23	Antichrist
2:24—3:24	What living as children of God means
4:1-6	The spirit of truth and the spirit of falsehood
4:7—5:12	Love, obedience and faith lead to victory.
5:13-21	Conclusion

The first epistle of John can serve as an excellent introduction to the climate of thought of the fourth Gospel and into the nature of Christianity as John saw it. For John, the foundation of all Christian truth is the Incarnation. To doubt that the Word has come in the flesh was the most fatal of all heresies.

In the
Old Testament

John, both in the Gospel and this epistle, places before us the choice between light and darkness, the choice for or against God, the "yes" or "no" to the call of God in Christ. The book of Deuteronomy, too, confronts us with a similar choice before the living God.

Read Deuteronomy 30.

In our life

The ideal of communal solidarity (salvation through the community) in the Old Testament is changed in John into, no more ties of blood, but ties of Christian love based on faith in Christ.

Points to think about

1. As you go through this epistle, highlight the lines and phrases where the apostle emphasizes the importance of the link between the Incarnation and fraternal love.

2. Reflect on 3:1-2—what it means to be a "child of God."

3. Note how both in language and ideas, 1 John resembles the Gospel of John.

4. Reflect how the expression, "God is love" (4:8) says much more than just "God loves." It implies that whatever God does, He does in love. When He creates, He creates in love. When He governs, He governs in love. Even His punishments are redemptive, as the prophet Hosea already said in the Old Testament.

5. The great lesson of this epistle is that Christian life must be a life of love (4:16), that is, a life that continues the pattern of love that God has shown us in Christ, especially, in the great event, the climax of salvation history: the death and resurrection of Christ, the Paschal Mystery.

Selections

1:1-10   God is life, God is light.
1:18-25 Warning against antichrist
3:11-18 Children of God
5:1-12   He who has the Son has life.

Prayer: Lord Jesus, we thank You and we praise You for the prayer You made for us to Your heavenly Father before You suffered: that all Christians may be one in You as the Father is in You and You in the Father (cf. Jn. 17:21). We pray that the grace of Your resurrection may realize this in us by the power of Your Holy Spirit. Amen.

Song: God is Love. Rivers. (OPPS - 282)

Thought for the day: If God so loves us, we also ought to love one another (1 John 4:12).

SECOND AND THIRD EPISTLES OF JOHN

"Anyone who...does not abide in the doctrine of Christ does not have God" (2 Jn. 9).

Second
epistle of John

The unnamed lady and her children to whom the letter is addressed signifies possibly the Church in another city. The letter calls for authentic Christian life, and a steadfast adherence to the teachings of Christ.

The epistle contains only 13 verses, eight of which are found in substance in the first. It contains no direct indication as to when or where it was written.

1-3   Greeting and introduction
4-6   The commandment of love and Christian life
7-11   Do not receive false teachers
12-13 Personal message and conclusion

Third
epistle of John

Third John is a personal letter to a gracious friend called Gaius, thanking him for giving hospitality to some Christian missionaries, and encouraging him on the way as a child of God.

1-2   Introduction
3-8   The traveling missionaries and Gaius
9-11   The bad example of Diotrephes
12   Approval of Demetrius
13-15 Conclusion

Prayer: Recite Psalm 36.

"With you is the fountain of life by your light we see the light" (JB).

Thought for the day: "Do not imitate evil, but imitate good" (3 Jn. 11).

REVELATION

A new heaven
and a new earth (21:1)

The hostility of the Roman empire did not end with the death of Nero on June 9th, 68 A.D. In the persecution of the autocratic emperor Domitian (c. A.D. 91-96), the infant Church was to experience a more terrible ordeal. Possibly about this time, a book appeared which was most likely a work of encouragement to the persecuted Christians (like the book of Daniel at the time of the Maccabees). According to many of the early Fathers of the Church, it is attributed to the aged apostle John, living at the time in exile on the little island off the coast of Greece called Patmos.

As we have seen in the book of Daniel, the author of Revelation seems to adopt the apocalyptic literary form in order to give spiritual encouragement and solace to the victims of persecution. Although evil seems to retain its power, there is no doubt as to the final issue. In this struggle between the forces of darkness and the forces of light, the cause of Christ and truth are assured of victory.

In the Old Testament

Much of the imagery, the metaphors, the figurative language and visions of this last book of the New Testament present a problem for the modern reader. But when read against the background of the books of the Old Testament, especially the prophets like Ezekiel and apocalyptic books like Daniel, Zechariah, etc., they are seen in a new light and become intelligible.

Read e.g., Isaiah chs. 24-27; Zechariah chs. 1-6 or Daniel ch. 12.

In our life

In facing the evils of our time, the strength that the "revelation" of Patmos gave the early Christians should inspire us with a similar indomitable faith in the final victory of Christ. It should also encourage us joyfully to make the contribution of our testimony and witness toward that final victory. In spite of all appearances to the contrary, human history has a meaning, and the Christian destiny is not one of death but of life.

Points to think about

1. In reading this book, a pitfall into which the reader can easily fall is to take these visions for realities or to wish to represent what John describes. His language is that of the apocalyptic writers, a language of images. So what is important is not so much to reproduce the images as to understand their meaning, to "translate" them. For example, eyes symbolize knowledge; wings = mobility; legs = stability; hands or horns = power and domination; a crown = the royalty of those who carry it; a long robe = priesthood; a palm = triumph; a bowl or cup = destruction and death; Babylon = Rome. The colors themselves can have a symbolic meaning; white = sign of joy, of purity, of victory; red or blood = sign of murder; scarlet = luxury and debauchery. As for numbers, the number 7 symbolizes perfection, the number 4 = the world; 12 = the Church, the New Israel and 1000 = a vast number of people.

2. For the same reasons the cosmic phenomena, described in 6:12-17, for example, need not necessarily be a vivid, literal description of the end of the world. In the tradition of the language employed by prophets of the Old Testament, various images are used to describe in a picturesque manner the "Day of the Lord" (the great interventions of God in human history).

3. Similarly the glorious reign of Christ and of the just for a thousand years (popularly known as the millennium), mentioned in 20:1-6, need not be taken literally but rather understood in a symbolic sense, like the rest of the visions of the book.

4. The important thing is to keep one's eyes on the general message of the book as stated above and understand the rest in the light of that message. Christianity is a religion of hope. This hope is not in man's ability but in God's sovereign power. Our failures are not God's failures (conversely, also, what we think are our successes, may not be necessarily in accordance with God's plans). Christian hope is rooted in faith in

the sovereign power and freedom of God to bring to fulfillment the plan He had in the creation of the world (Ep. 1:3f.). The mission of the Church is in relation to a God who is even now at work in history—in the present salvific moment.

5. It is significant that the Bible opens with the words: "In the beginning God created the heavens and the earth" (Gn. 1:1) and ends with the vision of the new heavens and the new earth which God will create at the end of time (Rv. ch. 21). The pages in between narrate the history of our salvation, the center of which is the mystery of Christ, the Savior.

Selections

Ch. 4	A vision of the glory of the risen Christ in heaven
Ch. 14	The Church triumphant
Ch. 18:1—19:10	The fall of the "great Babylon" and the victory of the Lamb
Ch. 21	A new heaven and a new earth

Prayer: Recite Rv. 4:11; 5:9; 19:7, 8.

Song: I saw the Holy City. Robert Blue. (HYC - I - 140)

Thought for the day: "Let him who is thirsty come, let him who desires, take the water of life without price" (22:17).

MY FAVORITE PASSAGES FROM THE GENERAL EPISTLES AND BOOK OF REVELATION:

Quiz on the General (or Catholic) Epistles and Revelation

1. Mark the correct answer: The number of the so-called general or Catholic epistles in the New Testament is a) 10   b) 7   c) 5

2. "But you are a chosen race, a royal priesthood, a holy nation, God's own people." Name the epistle wherein these words are found.

3. Mark the correct answer: The control of the tongue is particularly emphasized in
   1) 1 Peter
   2) James
   3) Jude

4. "...God is light and in him there is no darkness at all." From which epistle are these words taken?

5. The epistle that speaks of the archangel Michael contending with the devil about the body of Moses is:
   a) Revelation
   b) Jude

6. "And we have the prophetic word made more sure. You will do well to pay attention to this as to a lamp shining in a dark place until the day dawns and the morning star rises in your hearts."
   Where are these beautiful words found?

7. Which book speaks of the new heaven and the new earth?

8. Mark the correct answer: "...I saw a Lamb standing, as though it had been slain..." (Rv. 5:6). These words stand for: a) an angel
   b) the Church
   c) the risen Christ

9. "Be doers of the word and not hearers only."
   These words are from: 1) 1 Peter
   2) 1 John
   3) James

10. "And let him who is thirsty come, let him who desires take the water of life without price."
    Where can these words be found?

Answers on page 276.

Answers to all the quizzes

1. **Pentateuch**
    1. Torah (law or teaching)
    2. Right
    3. Chapter 12
    4. Death of the first-born
    5. (b)
    6. Epistle to the Hebrews
    7. Commentary
    8. Numbers ch. 6
    9. Deuteronomy ch. 26
   10. Chapter 24

2. **"Historical" books**
    1. The former Prophets
    2. Ruth to Naomi
    3. Solomon
    4. 2 S. 7
    5. Ahaz
    6. Israel
    7. Zedekiah
    8. (3)
    9. (1)
   10. Hannah, mother of Samuel (1 S. 2:1)

3. **Wisdom**
    1. Writings
    2. Proverbs (7:22)
    3. The problem of innocent suffering
    4. Ps. 110
    5. (b)
    6. Song of Solomon
    7. Qoheleth (12:1)
    8. Qoheleth
    9. Psalms (49:13-15)
   10. Qoheleth (3:1)

4. **Prophets**
    1. Isaiah
    2. Amos (5:24)
    3. (b)

  4. Jeremiah (31:31)
  5. Obadiah
  6. Habakkuk (2:4)
  7. Ezekiel (ch. 37)
  8. Joel 2:28 (RSV); 3:1 (JB and NAB)
  9. Daniel ch. 7
 10. Micah (6:8)

5. Gospels and Acts

  1. Luke
  2. Mark
  3. Wrong (Mt., Mk., Lk.)
  4. Luke
  5. John
  6. Matthew
  7. Luke
  8. Mark
  9. Matthew
 10. Feeding of the five thousand

6. "Pauline" Epistles

  1. Romans
  2. Galatians
  3. Ephesians (5:21-33)
  4. Colossians (3:1)
  5. Wrong
  6. (b)
  7. False
  8. Hebrews (11:1)
  9. 1 Corinthians (13:1)
 10. 1 Corinthians (ch. 15)

7. General (Catholic) Epistles and Revelation

  1. (b)
  2. 1 Peter (2:9)
  3. James ch. 3
  4. 1 John (1:5)
  5. Jude (v. 9)
  6. 2 Peter (1:19)
  7. Revelation (ch. 21)
  8. (c)
  9. James
 10. Revelation (22:17)

Keep a check on your Bible reading
(The BIBLE in chapters)

1. Remember, **how** one reads is more important than **how much** one reads.
2. Make a habit of daily reading and read it **meaningfully** with the help of this guide: what does it mean to me **today?**

OLD TESTAMENT

Pentateuch

Genesis								
1	**2**	**3**	4	5	6	7	8	9
10	11	**12**	13	14	15	16	**17**	18
19	20	21	**22**	23	24	25	26	27
28	29	30	31	32	33	34	35	36
37	38	39	40	41	42	43	44	45
46	47	48	49	50				

Exodus								
1	2	**3**	4	5	6	7	8	9
10	11	**12**	**13**	**14**	15	16	17	18
19	20	21	22	23	**24**	25	**26**	27
28	29	30	31	32	33	34	35	36
37	38	39	40					

Leviticus								
1	2	3	4	5	6	7	8	9
10	11	12	13	14	15	16	17	18
19	20	21	22	23	24	25	**26**	27

Numbers								
1	2	3	4	5	6	7	8	9
10	**11**	12	13	14	15	16	17	18
19	20	21	22	23	24	25	26	27
28	29	30	31	32	33	34	35	36

Deuteronomy								
1	2	3	4	5	6	7	8	9
10	11	12	13	14	15	16	17	18
19	20	21	22	23	24	25	**26**	27
28	29	**30**	31	32	33	34		

Narratives

Joshua									
1	2	3	4	5	6	7	8	9	
10	11	12	13	14	15	16	17	18	
19	20	21	22	23	**24**				

Judges									
1	**2**	3	4	5	6	7	8	9	
10	11	12	13	14	15	16	17	18	
19	20	21							

Ruth			
1	2	3	**4**

1 Samuel									
1	2	3	4	5	6	7	8	9	
10	11	12	13	14	15	**16**	17	18	
19	20	21	22	23	24	25	26	27	
28	29	30	31						

2 Samuel									
1	2	3	4	5	6	**7**	8	9	
10	11	**12**	13	14	15	16	17	18	
19	20	21	22	23	24				

1 Kings									
1	2	3	4	5	6	7	**8**	9	
10	11	12	13	14	15	16	17	18	
19	20	21	22						

2 Kings									
1	2	3	4	5	6	7	8	9	
10	11	12	13	14	15	16	**17**	18	
19	20	21	**22**	23	**24**	**25**			

1 Chronicles									
1	2	3	4	5	6	7	8	9	
10	11	12	13	14	15	16	**17**	18	
19	20	21	22	23	24	25	26	27	
28	29	30							

2 Chronicles									
1	2	3	4	**5**	**6**	**7**	8	9	
10	11	12	13	14	15	16	17	18	
19	20	21	22	23	24	25	26	27	
28	29	30	31	32	33	34	**35**	**36**	

Ezra									
1	2	3	4	**5**	**6**	7	8	9	
10									

Nehemiah	1 2 3 4 5 6 7 **8** **9**
	10 11 12 13

Tobit	1 2 3 4 5 6 7 8 9
	10 11 12 13 14

Judith	1 2 3 4 5 6 7 8 9
	10 11 12 13 14 15 16

Esther	1 2 3 4 5 6 7 8 9
	10

1 Maccabees	**1** 2 3 4 5 6 7 8 9
	10 11 12 13 14 15 16

2 Maccabees	1 2 3 4 5 6 **7** 8 9
	10 11 12 13 14 15

Wisdom

Job	1 2 **3** 4 5 6 7 8 9
	10 11 12 13 14 15 16 17 18
	19 20 21 22 23 24 25 26 27
	28 **29** **30** 31 32 33 34 35 36
	37 **38** **39** **40** **41** **42**

Psalms	**1** **2** 3 4 5 6 7
	8 9 10 11 12 13 14
	15 16 17 18 **19** 20 21
	22 **23** 24 25 26 **27** 28
	29 30 31 32 33 34 35
	36 **37** 38 39 40 41 42
	43 44 **45** 46 47 **48** **49**
	50 **51** 52 53 54 55 56
	57 58 59 60 61 **62** 63
	64 65 66 67 68 69 70
	71 72 **73** 74 75 76 77
	78 79 80 81 82 83 84
	85 86 **87** 88 89 **90** 91
	92 93 94 **95** 96 **97** **98**

99   100 101 102 **103 104 105**
106 107 108 109 **110** 111 112
113 114 115 116 117 118 **119**
120 121 122 123 124 125 126
127 128 129 130 131 **132** 133
134 **135 136 137** 138 **139** 140
141 142 143 144 145 146 147
148 149 150

Proverbs	**1** 2 3 4 5 6 7 **8** 9
	10 11 12 13 14 15 16 17 18
	19 20 21 22 23 24 25 26 27
	28 29 30 31

Qoheleth	**1** 2 3 4 5 6 7 8 9
	10 **11** 12

Song of Solomon	1 2 3 4 5 6 7 8

Wisdom	1 2 3 4 5 6 **7** 8 9
	10 11 12 13 14 15 16 17 18
	19

Sirach	1 2 3 4 5 6 7 8 9
	10 11 12 13 14 15 16 17 18
	19 20 21 22 23 **24** 25 26 27
	28 29 30 31 32 33 34 35 36
	37 38 39 40 41 42 43 44 45
	46 47 48 49 50 51

Prophecy

Isaiah	1 2 3 4 5 **6 7** 8 **9**
	10 **11** 12 13 14 15 16 17 18
	19 20 21 22 23 24 25 26 27

28	29	30	31	32	33	34	35	36
37	38	39	**40**	41	42	43	44	45
46	47	48	49	50	51	52	**53**	54
55	56	57	58	59	**60**	**61**	62	63
64	65	66						

Jeremiah								
1	**2**	3	4	5	6	7	8	9
10	11	12	13	14	15	16	17	18
19	20	21	22	23	24	25	26	27
28	29	30	**31**	32	33	34	35	36
37	38	39	40	41	42	43	44	45
46	47	48	49	50	51	52		

Lamentations				
1	2	3	4	5

Ezekiel								
1	2	3	4	5	6	7	8	9
10	11	12	13	14	15	16	17	18
19	20	21	22	23	24	25	26	27
28	29	30	31	32	33	**34**	35	**36**
37	38	39	40	41	42	43	44	45
46	47	48						

Daniel								
1	2	3	4	5	6	**7**	8	9
10	11	**12**						

Hosea								
1	**2**	3	4	5	6	7	8	9
10	11	12	13	14	15	16		

Joel			
1	2	**3**	4

Amos								
1	2	3	4	5	6	7	8	9

Obadiah
1

Jonah			
1	2	3	4

Micah						
1	2	3	4	5	6	7

Nahum		
1	2	3

Habakkuk		
1	2	3

Zephaniah		
1	2	3

Haggai	1	2							
Zechariah	1	2	3	4	5	6	7	8	9
	10	11	12	13	14	15	16		
Malachi	1	2	3	**4**					
<u>Baruch</u>	1	2	3	4	5	6			

NEW TESTAMENT

Gospels

Matthew	1	2	3	4	**5**	**6**	**7**	8	9
	10	11	12	13	14	15	16	17	18
	19	20	21	22	23	24	25	**26**	27
	28								

Mark	**1**	2	3	4	5	**6**	7	**8**	**9**
	10	11	12	13	14	15	16		

Luke	**1**	**2**	3	4	5	6	7	8	9
	10	11	12	13	14	**15**	16	17	18
	19	20	21	**22**	**23**	**24**			

John	**1**	2	**3**	**4**	5	**6**	7	**8**	9
	10	11	12	13	**14**	**15**	**16**	**17**	18
	19	20	21						

Acts	1	**2**	3	4	5	6	7	8	**9**
	10	11	12	**13**	14	15	16	17	18
	19	20	21	22	23	24	25	26	27
	28								

Pauline Epistles

Romans	**1**	2	3	4	**5**	**6**	7	**8**	9
	10	11	12	13	14	15	16		

1 Corinthians	1	2	3	4	5	6	7	8	9
	10	11	12	**13**	14	**15**	16		

2 Corinthians	1	2	3	4	**5**	6	7	8	9
	10	**11**	**12**	13					

Galatians	1	2	3	4	**5**	6

Ephesians	**1**	**2**	**3**	4	5	6

Philippians	1	2	3	4

Colossians	**1**	2	**3**	4					
1 Thessalonians	1	2	3	4	5				
2 Thessalonians	1	**2**	3						
1 Timothy	1	2	3	4	5	6			
2 Timothy	1	2	3	4					
Titus	1	2	3						
Philemon	1								
Hebrews	**1**	2	3	4	5	6	7	8	**9**
	10	11	12	13					

General (Catholic) Epistles

James	1	2	3	4	5				
1 Peter	**1**	**2**	3	4	5				
2 Peter	1	2	3						
1 John	**1**	2	3	4	5				
2 John	1								
3 John	1								
Jude	1								
Revelation	1	2	3	4	**5**	6	7	8	9
	10	11	12	13	14	15	16	17	18
	19	20	**21**	**22**					

Select Bibliography (Optional)

GENERAL AND INTRODUCTORY

1. Paul VI, Pope. "Address to Professors of Holy Scripture," Sept. 25, 1970. L'Osservatore Romano, Oct. 8, 1970.
2. Pius XII, Pope. Encyclical on Holy Scripture, "Divino Afflante Spiritu." Sept. 38, 1943. AAS. 38. 1943. pp. 297-326.
3. The Second Vatican Council. Dogmatic Constitution on Divine Revelation, "Dei Verbum." Boston: St. Paul Editions.
4. Charlier, C. **The Christian Approach to the Bible.** Maryland: Newman Press, 1958.
5. Levy, Jean. **The Word of God in the Words of Men.**
6. Brown, R. E., ed. **The Jerome Biblical Commentary.** London: Chapman, 1968.
7. **Peake's Commentary on the Bible.** New York: Nelson and Sons, 1962.
8. **The Interpreter's Bible** in 12 vols. New York: Abingdon Press.
9. **A New Catholic Commentary on Holy Scripture.** New Jersey: Thomas Nelson and Sons, 1969.
10. **Old Testament Reading Guide.** Collegeville: Liturgical Press.

THE OLD TESTAMENT

1. Genesis

1. Von Rad, G. "Genesis," **Old Testament Library.** Westminster, 1961. esp. pp. 149ff.
2. Bright, John. "History of Israel," ch. 2, **Old Testament Library.** London: SCM Press, Ltd., 1964.
3. Cornfeld, Gaalyahu. **Adam to Daniel.** New York: The Macmillan Co., 1962.
4. Anderson, Bernhard W. **Understanding the Old Testament.** New Jersey: Prentice Hall, 1957.

5. Albright, G. F. **From the Stone Age to Christianity.** Garden City, New York: Doubleday Anchor Books, 1957. esp. pp. 200-243.
6. Thomas, D. Winton, ed. **Documents from Old Testament.** London: Times, 1958.

2. Exodus

1. **The Bible Today:**
   (1) Lynch, William E. "The Eucharist: A Covenant Meal." 1962-1963. Vol. 1, 318-323.
   (2) Wood, Geoffrey. "The Eucharist, the New Passover Meal." 1962-1963. Vol. 1, 310-317.
   (3) Maly, Eugene H. "The Paschal Sacrifice, Old and New." Vol. 3, 852-857.
2. Plastaras, James. **The God of the Exodus.** Milwaukee: Bruce, 1966. esp. ch. 14: "Exodus Themes in the New Testament."
3. Bright, John. **A History of Israel.** esp. ch. 3. London: SCM Press, Ltd., 1964.
4. Beegle, Dewey, M. **Moses, the Servant of Yahweh.** Grand Rapids, Mich.: Eerdmans, 1972.
5. **The Sixteen Documents of Vatican II.** Boston: St. Paul Editions.

3. Leviticus

1. Noth, Martin. "Leviticus," **Old Testament Library.** Philadelphia, 1965.
2. Vatican Council II, Dogmatic Constitution on the Church, "Lumen gentium." **The Sixteen Documents of Vatican II.** Boston: St. Paul Editions.

4. Numbers

1. "The Book of Numbers," **Worship.** 31. 1957. 592-600.
2. **Old Testament Reading Guide.** Collegeville, 1965.

5. **Deuteronomy**

   1. Brown, R. E. **Old Testament Reading Guide.** Collegeville, 1965.
   2. Wright, G. Ernest. **Interpreter's Bible,** vol. II. New Jersey: Abingdon Press, 1953. (This is one of the best.)
   3. Lohfink, N. "In Verbum Domini," 41. 1963. 73-77.
   4. Von Rad, G. "Deuteronomy." London, 1966.
   5. Myers, J. M. "On the Theology of Deuteronomy," **Interpretation.** 15. 1961. 14-31.

6. **The book of Joshua**

   1. Bright, John. "The Book of Joshua," **Interpreter's Bible.** New York, 1953.
   2. Rowley, H. H. **From Joseph to Joshua.** London, 1950.

7. **The book of Judges**

   1. Mackenzie, J. L. **The World of the Judges.** New Jersey, 1966.
   2. Robertson, ·E. "The Period of the Judges: A Mystery Period in the History of Israel." Bulletin of the John Rylands Library, 30 (1946) 91-114.

8. **The book of Ruth**

   1. Loretz, O. "The Theme of the Ruth Story," **Catholic Biblical Quarterly,** 22 (1960) 391-99.
   2. Burrows, M. "The Marriage of Boaz and Ruth," **Journal of Biblical Literature,** 59 (1940) 445-54.

9. **The books of Samuel**

   1. **Old Testament Reading Guide.** Collegeville, 1965.
   2. Brockington, L. "1 and 2 Samuel," **Peake's Commentary.** London, 1962.

10. **The books of Kings 1 and 2**

   1. Maly, Eugene H. **The World of David and Solomon.** Englewood Cliffs, N.J.: Prentice-Hall, 1965.

2. Swanston, H. F. G. **The Kings and the Covenant.** London, 1967.

11. **The books of Chronicles 1 and 2**

1. North, R. "Theology of the Chronicles," **Journal of Biblical Literature,** 82. 1963. 369-381.
2. Myers, J. "1 and 2 Chronicles," **The Anchor Bible.** Garden City, N.Y.: Doubleday & Co., 1965.

12. **Ezra-Nehemiah**

1. Torrey, C. C. "The Chronicler's History of Israel, Chronicles - Ezra - Nehemiah Restored to Its Original Form," **Old Testament Reading Guide.** New Haven: Yale University Press, 1954.
2. Myers, J. M. "Ezra - Nehemiah," **The Anchor Bible.** Garden City, N.Y.: Doubleday & Co., 1965.

13. **The book of Tobit**
Dumm, D. R. "Tobit," **The Jerome Biblical Commentary.** Englewood Cliffs, N.J.: Prentice-Hall, 1968.

14. **The book of Judith**
Dumm, D. R. "Judith," **The Jerome Biblical Commentary.** Englewood Cliffs, N.J.: Prentice-Hall, 1968.

15. **The book of Esther**

Dumm, D. R. "Esther," **The Jerome Biblical Commentary.** Englewood Cliffs, N.J.: Prentice-Hall, 1968.

16. **The books of the Maccabees 1 and 2**

1. Tedesche, S. and Zeitlin, S. "The First Book of Maccabees," **Old Testament Reading Guide.** N.Y., 1950. "The Second Book of Maccabees," **Old Testament Reading Guide.** N.Y., 1954.
2. Pfeiffer, R. H. **History of New Testament Times.** New York, N.Y.: Harper Bros., 1949. p. 485.

17. The book of Job

1. Terrien, S. **Job, Poet of Existence.** Indianapolis, 1957.
2. Skehan, P. W. "Strophic Patterns in the Book of Job," **Catholic Biblical Quarterly,** 23. 1961. 125-142.
3. Terrien, S. "Introduction and Exegesis of Job," **Interpreter's Bible.** Abingdon, 1954.
4. Peake, Arthur S. **The Problem of Suffering in the Old Testament.** ch. 5. London, 1947.

18. The book of Psalms

1. Terrien, Samuel. **The Psalms and Their Meaning for Today.** Indianapolis, Ind.: Bobbs-Merrill, 1952.
2. Weiser, Artur. **The Psalms.** Philadelphia, Pa., 1962.
3. Mowinckel, S. **The Psalms in Israel's Worship.** Vols. 1 and 2. New York, 1962.
4. Ringgren, H. **The Faith of the Psalmists.** London, 1963.

19. The book of Proverbs

1. Murphy, R. E. **Seven Books of Wisdom.** Milwaukee. 1960.
2. Skehan, P. W. "The Seven Columns of Wisdom": "House in Proverbs," **Catholic Biblical Quarterly.** 10(1948)115-130 and 29(1967)468-86.
3. Scott, R. B. Y. "Proverbs," **Anchor Bible,** New York, 1965.

20. Qoheleth

1. Murphy, R. E. "Ecclesiastes (Qoheleth)," **Jerome Biblical Commentary.** Englewood Cliffs, N.J., 1968.
2. Gordis, Robert. **Qoheleth, the Man and His World.** New York: New York Jewish Theological Seminary of America Press, 1951.

21. The Canticle of Canticles (Song of Songs)

1. Murphy, R. E., "Canticle of Canticles," **Jerome Biblical Commentary.** New Jersey: Prentice-Hall, 1968.
2. Rowley, H. H. "The Interpretation of the Song of Songs," in the collected essays, **The Servant of the Lord and other essays on the Old Testament.** Oxford: Blackwell, 1965. pp. 195-245.
3. Bernard, St. **On the Song of Songs** (84 Sermons). All of the sermons are of great depth and beauty.

22. The Wisdom of Solomon

1. Wright, Addison G. "Wisdom," **Jerome Biblical Commentary.** New Jersey: Prentice-Hall, 1968.
2. Geyer, J. "The Wisdom of Solomon," **Torch Biblical Commentaries.** London, 1963.
3. Pfeiffer, R. H. **History of New Testament Times.** New York, N.Y.: Harper and Bros., 1949.

23. Sirach (Ecclesiasticus)

1. Weber, Thomas H. "Sirach," **Jerome Biblical Commentary.** New Jersey: Prentice-Hall, 1968.
2. Vawter, B. **The Book of Sirach.** Paulist Bible Pamphlet Series. New York, 1962.

24. Isaiah 1-39

1. Moriarty, F. L. "Isaiah, 1-39," **Jerome Biblical Commentary.** New Jersey: Prentice-Hall, 1968.
2. Vriezen, Th. C. "Essentials of the Theology of Isaiah," **Israel's Prophetic Heritage.** B. W. Anderson and Walter Harrelson, ed. New York: Harper & Row, 1962.
3. Scott, R. B. Y. "Introduction and Exegesis to Isaiah," **Interpreter's Bible.** New York: Abingdon Press, 1956.

25. Isaiah 40-66

1. North, R. Christopher. **Isaiah 40-55.** New York: Macmillan, 1966.

2. Rowley, H. H. **The Servant of the Lord and Other Essays on the Old Testament.** Oxford: Blackwell, 1965. pp. 3-60.
3. Anderson, B. W. "Exodus Typology in Second Isaiah," **Israel's Prophetic Heritage.** New York: Harper & Row, 1962.
4. Zimmerli, Walter and Jeremias, J. "The Servant of God," **Studies in Biblical Theology,** no. 20. London: SCM Press, 1957.

26. **Jeremiah**

1. Bright, John. "Jeremiah," **Anchor Bible.** New York: Doubleday, 1965.
2. Hyatt, Philip J. **Jeremiah, Prophet of Courage and Hope.** New York: Abingdon Press, 1958.
3. Anderson, B. W. **The Old Testament and Christian Faith** (on Jeremiah 3:31-34). New York: Harper & Row, 1963. pp. 225-242.
4. Muilenburg, J. "Jeremiah, the Prophet," **Interpreter's Dictionary of the Bible.** Nashville, 1963, pp. 823-835.

27. **Ezekiel**

1. Rowley, H. H. **The Book of Ezekiel in Modern Study.** Manchester: University Press, 1953.
2. May, Herbert G. "Introduction and Exegesis to Ezekiel," **Interpreter's Bible.** New York: Abingdon Press, 1956.
3. Ackroyd, Peter R. **Exile and Restoration.** Philadelphia, 1968.
4. Eisfeldt, Otto. "The Prophetic Literature," **The Old Testament and Modern Study.** H. H. Rowley, ed. pp. 153-158.

28. **Daniel**

1. Hartman, C.S.S.R., Louis F. "Daniel," **The Jerome Biblical Commentary.** New Jersey, 1968.
2. Rowley, H. H. **The Relevance of Apocalyptic,** 2nd ed. London: Lutterworth Press. 1947.

29. Hosea

1. McKenzie, J. "Divine Passion in Osee," **Catholic Biblical Quarterly** 17(1955), pp. 287-299.
2. Ward, J. M. **Hosea: A Theological Commentary.** New York, 1966.
3. Rowley, H. H. "The Marriage of Hosea," Bulletin of the John Rylands Library, 39, 1 (1956), pp. 200-233.

30. Joel

1. Bentzen, Aage. **Introduction to the Old Testament,** vol. 2. Copenhagen: GAD Publisher, 1967. p. 134f.
2. Pfeiffer, R. H. **Introduction to the Old Testament.** New York: Harper & Bros., 1941. p. 575ff.
3. Thompson, J. A. "Joel," **Interpreter's Bible.** New York: Abingdon Press, 1956.

31. Amos

1. Terrien, Samuel. "Amos and Wisdom," **Israel's Prophetic Heritage.** B. W. Anderson and Walter Harrelson, ed. New York: Harper & Bros., 1962. pp. 108-115.
2. Von Rad, G. **The Message of the Prophets.** London: SCM Press.

32. Obadiah

Wood, Geoffrey. "Obadiah," **Jerome Biblical Commentary.** New Jersey, 1968.

33. Jonah

1. Stanton, G. B., "The Prophet Jonah and His Message," **Bibliotheca Sacra.** 108(1951) 237-249, 363-376.
2. **The Sixteen Documents of Vatican II.** Boston: St. Paul Editions.

34. Micah

1. Copass, B. and Carlson, E. **Study of Prophet Micah.** Grand Rapids, 1950.
2. Snaith, N. **Amos, Hosea, Micah.** London, 1956.

35. Nahum

Murphy, O.P., Richard T. A. "Zephaniah, Nahum, Habakkuk," **The Jerome Biblical Commentary.** New Jersey, 1968.

36. Habakkuk

Murphy, O.P., Richard T. A., **op. cit.**

37. Zephaniah

Murphy, O.P., Richard T. A., **op. cit.**

38. Zechariah

1. Thomas, D. Winton. "The Book of Zechariah, 1-8," **Interpreter's Bible.** 1956.
2. Dentan, R. C. "The Book of Zechariah, 9-14," **Interpreter's Bible.** 1956.
3. May, H. G. "A Key to the Interpretation of Zechariah's Visions," **Journal of Biblical Literature.** 57(1958)173-184.

39. Malachi

1. Dentan, R. C. "The Book of Malachi," **Interpreter's Bible,** 1956.
2. Robinson, A. "God the Refiner of Silver," **Catholic Biblical Quarterly.** 11(1949), pp. 188-190.

THE NEW TESTAMENT

1. The Gospel according to Matthew

1. Dupont, J. **Les Beatitudes.** Bruges, 1958.
2. Vann, Gerald. **The Divine Pity: A Study in the Social Implications of the O. P. Beatitudes.** New York: Sheed and Ward, 1946.
3. Davies, W. D. **The Setting of the Sermon on the Mount.** Cambridge, 1964.
4. Dodd, C. H. **The Parables of the Kingdom.** 1935.
5. Bruce, F. F. **The New Testament Development of Old Testament Themes.** Grand Rapids, Mich.: B. Eerdmans Publishing Co.

2. The Gospel according to Mark

1. Taylor, V. **The Gospel According to St. Mark.** 2nd ed. London, 1966.
2. Freyne, Sean and Wansbrough, Henry. **Mark and Matthew, Scripture Discussion Commentary.** Chicago: Acta, 1971.
3. Burkill, T. A. **Mysterious Revelation.** Ithaca, 1963.

3. The Gospel according to Luke

1. Stuhlmueller, C. P. Carroll. "The Gospel According to St. Luke," **The Jerome Biblical Commentary.** New Jersey, 1968.
2. Lampe, G. W. H. "Luke," **Peake's Commentary on the Bible** (revised edition). London, 1962.
3. Conzelmann, H. **The Theology of St. Luke.** New York, 1960.
4. Cadbury, H. J. **The Making of Luke - Acts** (2nd ed.). London, 1958.
5. Flender, H. **St. Luke, Theologian of Redemptive History.** Philadelphia, 1967.

4. The Gospel according to John

1. Brown, R. E. "The Gospel According to St. John and the Johannine Apostles," **Anchor Bible.** 29, Garden City, N.Y., 1966.

2. Dodd, C. H. **The Interpretation of the Faith Gospel.** Cambridge, 1953.
3. Schnackenburg, R. **The Gospel According to St. John.** Tr. Kevin Smith. New York: Herder and Herder, 1968.
4. Barrett, C. K. **The Gospel According to St. John.** London, 1959.

5. The Acts of the Apostles

1. Dillon, R. J. and Fitzmyer, S. J., Joseph A., "Acts of the Apostles," **Jerome Biblical Commentary.** New Jersey, 1968.
2. Dupont, J. **The Sources of Acts: The Present Position.** London, 1964.
3. O'Neill, J. C. **The Theology of Acts in Its Historical Setting.** London, 1961.

6. The epistle of Paul to the Romans

1. Lyonnet, S. **Epitre aux Romains.** Paris, 1954.
2. Fitzmyer, S.J., Joseph A., "Letter to the Romans," **Jerome Biblical Commentary.** New Jersey, 1968.
3. Dodd, C. H. "The Epistle of Paul to the Romans," **Mofatt New Testament Commentaries.**

7. Corinthians

1. He'ring, J. **The First Epistle of St. Paul to the Corinthians.** London, 1962.
2. Tasker, R. **The Second Epistle of Paul to the Corinthians.** Grand Rapids, 1958.
3. Thrall, M. E. "1 and 2 Corinthians," **Cambridge Bible Commentary, New English Bible.** 1965.

8. Galatians

1. Lyonnet, S. **Les Epitres de Saint Paul aux Galates, aux Romains** (2nd ed.) Paris, 1959.
2. Tenney, M. C. **Galatians, the Charter of Christian Liberty.** Grand Rapids, 1950.

9. Colossians, Philippians, Ephesians

1. Benoit, P. **Les Epitres de Saint Paul aux Phillipiens, a Philemon, aux Colossians, aux Ephesiens.** Paris, 1959.
2. Grassi, M.M., Joseph A. "The Letter to the Colossians," **Jerome Biblical Commentary.** New Jersey, 1968.
3. Grassi, M.M., Joseph A. "The Letter to the Ephesians," **Jerome Biblical Commentary.** New Jersey, 1968.
4. Fitzmyer, S.J., Joseph. A., "The Letter to the Philippians," **Jerome Biblical Commentary.** New Jersey, 1968.
5. Cerfaux, L. **The Church in the Theology of St. Paul.** New York, 1959.
6. Moule, F.E. **The Epistle to the Colossians and to Philemon.**

10. 1 and 2 Thessalonians

1. Vawter, B. "1 Thessalonians"; "2 Thessalonians," **New Testament Reading Guide.** 6. Collegeville, 1960.
2. Morris, L. "The First and Second Epistles to the Thessalonians," **New International Commentary on the New Testament.** Grand Rapids, 1959.

11. The pastoral epistles to Timothy and Titus

1. Denzer, George A. "The Pastoral Letters," **Jerome Biblical Commentary.** New Jersey, 1968.
2. Gealy, F. "The First and Second Epistles to Timothy and the Epistle to Titus," **Interpreter's Bible.** 11. New York, 1955.

12. Epistle to the Hebrews

1. Spicq, C. **L'Epitre aux Hebreux.** 2 volumes. Paris, 1953.
2. Vanhoye, A. **The Literary Structure of the Epistle to the Hebrews.** 1963.
3. Bourke, Myles M. "The Epistle to the Hebrews," **Jerome Biblical Commentary.** New Jersey, 1968.

4. Bruce, F. F. "The Epistle to the Hebrews," **New International Commentary on the New Testament.** Grand Rapids, 1964.

13. James

1. Leahy, S.J., Thomas W., "The Epistle of James," **Jerome Biblical Commentary.** New Jersey, 1968.
2. Reicke, B. "The Epistles of James, Peter and Jude," **Anchor Bible.** New York, 1964.

14. First epistle of Peter

1. Boismard, M. E. **Quatre Hymnes Baptismal dans L'Epitre de Pierre.** Editions du Cerf, 1961.
2. Ranpuet, P. G. **Baptismal Consecration and Religious Consecration.** Feurus, 1965.
3. Cantinat, J. "The First Epistle of Peter," **Introduction to the New Testament.** A. Robert and A. Feuillet, ed. New York, 1965.

15. The second epistle of Peter and the epistle of Jude

1. Reicke, B. "Epistles of James, Peter and Jude," **Anchor Bible.** 37. Garden City, N.Y., 1964.
2. Cantinat, J. "The Second Epistle of Peter and the Epistle of St. Jude," **Introduction to the New Testament.** A. Robert and A. Feuillet, ed. New York, 1965. pp. 582-600.

16. First epistle of John

1. Brown, R. E. "The Gospel According to St. John and the Johannine Epistles," **Anchor Bible.** 29. Garden City, N.Y., 1966.
2. Dodd, C. H. **The Johannine Epistles.** London: Hodder and Stoughton Ltd., 1961.

17. Revelation

1. Feuillet, A. **The Apocalypse.** Staten Island, N.Y., 1964.
2. Boismard, M. E. "The Apocalypse," **Introduction to the New Testament.** New York: Desclée Company. 1965.

Useful tools for the Bible student

1. Study Bibles

New American Bible (with notes). New Jersey, St. Anthony Guild Press.

The Jerusalem Bible (with notes), bound edition. London, Darton Longman & Todd, 1966. Garden City, New York, Doubleday & Company, Inc., 1966.

The Oxford Annotated Bible (Revised Standard Version). New York, Oxford Univ. Press, 1962.

Holman Study Bible (RSV). Philadelphia, A. J. Holman, 1962.

2. Concordances

The Oxford Concise Concordance to the RSV of the Holy Bible. New York, Oxford Univ. Press, 1962.

Leon-Dufour, X., **Concordance of the Synoptic Gospels.** R. O'Connel, tr. New York: Desclée, 1957.

3. Bible Dictionaries and Encyclopedias

McKenzi, S.J., John L. **Dictionary of the Bible.** New York, Bruce Publishing Co., 1965.

Buttrick, George A., ed. **Interpreter's Dictionary of the Bible.** New York, Abingdon Press, 1962.

4. Bible Geographies and Atlases

Rowley, H. H. **The Modern Reader's Bible Atlas.** (pocket size). New York, Association Press, 1961.

Some Useful Terms

1. **Canon of the Bible:** The authoritative list of the books that make up the Bible.
2. **Deuterocanonical:** The name designates those books of the Bible whose place in the Canon was at some time disputed or doubted in the Church.
3. **Inspiration:** This term is generally taken to signify the divine origin of the books of the Bible.
4. **Inerrancy:** A consequence of inspiration, which guarantees the absence of error in the inspired books in matters that regard our salvation.
5. **Revelation:** God's manifestation of Himself to His creatures.
6. **Septuagint:** The Jewish "Greek Version" of the Old Testament made before the Christian era.
7. **Vulgate:** The Latin version of the Bible made by St. Jerome on the mandate of Pope Damascus (382 A.D.).

THE ENTIRE
BIBLE
AT A GLANCE

what is
the
Bible?

It is the Word of God—
the story of our salvation

Its central theme is the **Mystery of Christ**
hidden in God from all eternity,
prepared for in the history of the Chosen People
(Old Testament)
and manifested to us in the fullness of time
(New Testament)

The Word of God is not a **problem** to be solved
but a **mystery** to be **lived!**

Old Testament
(The Sinai Covenant)

46 Books, written during a period of several centuries, of which

1 are "narratives"	18 are called the "prophets"	7 are called "wisdom" books

. Genesis ⎫ The "Pentateuch"
. Exodus ⎬ or
. Leviticus ⎭ "Torah" (law)
. Numbers
. Deuteronomy
. Joshua
. Judges
. Ruth
. 1 Samuel
0. 2 Samuel
1. 1 Kings
2. 2 Kings
3. 1 Chronicles
4. 2 Chronicles
5. Ezra
6. Nehemiah
7. 1 Maccabees
8. 2 Maccabees
9. Tobit
0. Judith
1. Esther
	1. Isaiah
	2. Jeremiah
	3. Ezekiel
	4. Daniel
	5. Hosea
	6. Joel
	7. Amos
	8. Obadiah
	9. Lamentation
	10. Jonah
	11. Micah
	12. Nahum
	13. Habakkuk
	14. Zephaniah
	15. Haggai
	16. Zechariah
	17. Malachi
	18. Baruch
		1. Job
		2. Psalms
		3. Proverbs
		4. Ecclesiastes
		   (Qoheleth)
		5. Song of Songs
		6. Wisdom
		7. Ecclesiasticus
		   (Sirach)

The first 5 narratives are called "The 5 books of Moses,"
the Torah or Pentateuch.

1. Genesis	—the origins of the world
	   mankind, pre-history (chs. 1-11)
	—the origins of the
	   Chosen People (next 39 chs.)
	
	A long "Prologue" to the story of
		Message:
		1. Mankind needed a Savio[r]
		2. God chose a people
		   to prepare His coming.
		
		the Exodus
		and
		the Sinai Covenant

2. Exodus	—God's saving act
	   (the Exodus from slavery)
	—the Covenant at Mt. Sinai
	
	first 18 chapters = narrative
	next 22 chapters = mainly laws
	
	The central event of the
	   Old Testament
		Message:
		God reveals Himself in this
		great saving act and in the
		Covenant.

3. Leviticus	—More laws and regulations —Holy Days first 7 chapters = Law of sacrifice next 3 chapters = the priesthood next 6 chapters = "clean" and "unclean" next 10 chapters = the holiness code Dedication of national life	**Message:** Consecration to God means holiness of life

4. Numbers	—census of people
	—the wandering in the wilderness
	
	first 4 chapters and 26 = census
	other chapters = narrative
	
	Second lap of the journey to the
	   Promised Land. (The murmurings
	   of Israel.)
		Message:
		Importance of faithfulness
		and perseverance

5. Deuteronomy	—Moses' last "discourses" —repeats laws first 11 chapters = Moses' spee[c]h 12-26 = revised laws 27-30 = closing speech 31-36 = conclusion of the Pentateuch The deeper meaning of the "Covenant"	**Message:** Religion is inseparable from life.

12 books make up the rest of the narratives	mostly on the history of the Chosen People right up to New Testament times.

Including 6 that are sometimes called the "former prophets" (history seen in the light of the prophets' teaching).

1. Joshua	2. Judges	3. 1 Samuel
—Joshua, successor of Moses as leader of God's people in the "conquest" of the Promised Land	—troubles in the land which called for local and national heroes ("Judges") —preface to the monarchical period	—toward the establishment of a monarchy in Israel —Saul —David
Message: God's saving action continues. Joshua, which means "God saves," becomes in Greek, "Jesus."	**Message:** Consequences of the infidelity of the people	**Message:** God's anointed one

4. 2 Samuel	5. 1 Kings	6. 2 Kings
—David —Jerusalem, symbol of united Israel	—Solomon —at his death, the division of the kingdom	—parallel account of the two kingdoms —down to the exile
Message: From now on Israel would look forward to a "New David," the Messiah.	**Message:** Division = the consequence of sin	**Message:** Sin = the root cause of the failure of the monarchy

And after the "exile" (586 B.C.—538 B.C.):

7 and 8	9 and 10	11 and 12
1 and 2 Chronicles —a review of the history of Israel	Ezra and Nehemiah —the return from exile —the re-organization of the community	1 and 2 Maccabees —religious persecution —martyrs for the faith
Message: The 2 sources of Israel's hope: the temple in her midst, and the messianic hope in the promise made to David (2 S. 7)	**Message:** The Jews = a people with a spiritual mission.	**Message:** God's kingdom is not of this world.

20. Reading the Bible

4 "Major" Prophets

1. Isaiah (the latter part of the eighth century B.C.)
 	
1-39 —oracles against Judah
      —against other nations
40-66—the dawn of a new age
 	
Message:
   1-39 God's holiness
   40-66 A light to the nations
	2. Jeremiah (c. 626 B.C. till the fall of Jerusalem)
	
	—last appeal to the nation in crisis
	—during 40 turbulent years preceding the exile
	
	Message:
	—The Old Covenant is to be replaced by a new covenant (31:31-34).

3. Ezekiel (c. 597 B.C. into the exile)
 	
—by the waters of Babylon
—can these bones live? (ch. 37)
 	
Message:
—inner conversion (36:26)
—an eternal covenant of peace (37:26)
	4. Daniel (c. 168 B.C.—Persecution of Antiochus IV Epiphanes)
	
	—a cryptic message of encouragement to a persecuted people
	
	Message:
	   —History has a meaning.
	   —God is the Lord of history (ch. 7).

and 14 "Minor" Prophets

5. Hosea (about the middle of the eighth century in the Northern Kingdom)
 	
—Israel's idolatry is a kind of adultery
 	
Message:
   God is a God of love and mercy
	6. Joel (probably sometime after the return from exile c. 450 B.C.)
	
	—a locust plague = a picture of divine judgment
	—call to repentance and prayer
	
	Message:
	   The outpouring of the spirit on all mankind in messianic times (3:1-5)

7. Amos (before Hosea in the Northern Kingdom)
 	
—Israel warned of coming disaster: capture of Samaria, 721 B.C.
 	
Message:
   "Let justice flow down like waters" (5:24)
	8. Obadiah (Some time after the fall of Jerusalem in 586 B.C.)
	
	—the guilt of Edom
	—she joined the enemies of her sister nation
	
	Message:
	   "For the violence done to your brother Jacob" (v. 10)

9. Jonah (during the period after the return from exile)

—the unwilling prophet to a pagan people

Message:
Beyond frontiers of race and religion: universality of God's salvation

10. Micah (about the time of Isaiah)

—Judah (the Southern kingdom) warned of coming disaster

Message:
Jerusalem will become a heap of ruins (3:12).

11. Nahum (fall of Nineveh, 612 B.C.)

—a cry of relief
—the end of a tyranny

Message:
The inevitable judgment of God that awaits all tyrants

12. Habakkuk (probably a little before Jeremiah)

—a prophet's problem: the problem of evil
—after Nineveh, now Babylon!

Message:
The righteous man will live by his faithfulness (2:4)

13. Zephaniah (about the time of Jeremiah)

—the "day of the Lord" is very near
—idolatry and sin = cause of the impending exile (597 B.C. onwards)

Message:
"She (Jerusalem) would never listen to the call, never learn the lesson" (3:2) (JB).

14. Haggai (just after the return from exile c. 520 B.C.)

—collect the broken stones and rebuild the temple of the Lord
—to the Jews returned from exile

Message:
Keeping the faith in a tedious time

15. Zechariah (1-8 with Haggai; 9-14 later!)

—rebuild the temple (1-8)
—messianic restoration centered on Jerusalem (9-14)

Message:
The power of hope

16. Malachi (perhaps preceded the reforms of Ezra and Nehemiah)

—a plea for sincerity in worship

Message:
True cult

17. Baruch (post-exilic period)

—the splendors of monotheism

Message:
The future glory of Jerusalem

18. Lamentations (on the fall of Jerusalem)

—How could it ever have happened!

Message:
Repentance and hope

and 4 edifying narratives

1. Ruth (about the same time as Jonah, after the exile) —the story of Ruth, the Moabitess who became David's great grandmother **Message:** The universality of God's call to salvation	2. Judith (post-exilic) —the extraordinary deliverance of the Jewish people through the hands of a woman **Message:** God never abandons His people
3. Tobit (post-exilic) —a pious Jewish family in exile —the struggle to live up to its ideals **Message:** God's Providence in daily life	4. Esther (post-exilic) —the deliverance of a section of the Jewish people from extermination —by the mediation of Esther —the origin of the feast of Purim **Message:** In every crisis, God is there to save, if only we pray

7 books make up "Wisdom" or "Reflective literature" (Proverbs, poetry, prayer)

1. Psalms (before, during and after the exile)

—the prayer book of the people of God

Message:
It is good to give thanks to the Lord (Ps. 90)

---

2. Job (about 450 B.C.—after the exile)

—the problem of innocent suffering

Message:
Man must learn to adore even when he cannot understand

3. Proverbs (before and after the exile)

—Collections of maxims and sayings

Message:
The fear of the Lord is the beginning of wisdom (1:1)

---

4. Ecclesiastes (Qoheleth) (post-exilic—Persian period)

—the human condition

Message:
Outside (of God) all is emptiness

5. Song of Songs (post-exilic)

—a poem of love

Message:
My beloved is mine and I am his—until the day dawns and the shadows flee away (2:16)

---

6. Wisdom (first century B.C.)

—the wisdom which comes from God

Message:
"Wisdom" was with God before the creation of the world and came forth from God (7:25-28).

7. Ecclesiasticus (Sirach) (about 180 B.C.)

—a lifelong meditation on God's law

Message:
The fear of the Lord is the perfection of wisdom

New Testament

The Good News about our Lord
             and Savior Jesus Christ:

The Gospels reveal the mystery of Christ,
which was prepared for
through the long ages
in the Old Testament.

The epistles explain to us this mystery
and apply it to our daily lives.

the 4 Gospels   "Gospel" means
                 "Good News"

N.B. The written Gospels were preceded by the spoken
     Gospel: the preaching of the apostles (eye-wit-
     nesses).

1. Matthew   —Jesus fulfilled the hope of the Old Testa-
(About   ment about the Messiah to come
70 A.D.)
             —Christians are the New People of God

             Message: The Gospel = the beginning of the
                          kingdom of God.

---

2. Mark   —Who is this man? The Messiah.
(Late   —What kind of Messiah? The "Son of Man."
sixties)   **Message:** The good news about Jesus Christ,
                         the Son of God.

---

3. Luke   —Joy to the world, to Jew and gentile, men
(Late   and women, sinner and saint, rich
seventies)   and poor.

             Message: Christianity = a world-religion,
                         transcending in its universality
                         all races and national limitations

---

4. John   —The total meaning of the life of Christ

(Early   **Message:** Christ is eternally present now
nineties)   acting through His Church. So
                         live, right now, the life of the
                         Risen Jesus through His Spirit in
                         the Church of the living God.

The Acts   —The early Church; especially the activ-
(After the   ity of the two great apostles, Peter and
Gospel of   Paul
Luke)

             Message: "You shall be witnesses unto me
                         to the ends of the earth."

14 "Letters of Paul"

	1. Romans (about 57-58 A.D.) —the meaning of Christianity **Message:** The Gospel is the power of God for salvation for everyone who believes (1:16).	2. 1 Corinthians (about 54 A.D.) —advice on the problems of the Corinthian Church **Message:** The standards of the kingdom
3. 2 Corinthians (about 54 A.D.) — continues the theme of 1 Corinthians — Paul's apostolic work — collection for the poor in Jerusalem **Message:** What Paul believes, he lives.	4. Galatians (c. 48 or c. 54 A.D.) —Judaism and Christianity **Message:** "When Christ freed us, he meant us to remain free" (5:1).	5. Ephesians (61-63 A.D.) —the mystery of salvation and the mystery of the Church **Message:** "Before the foundation of the world— God chose us in Christ" (1:6).
6. Philippians (c. 54 or c. 61-63 A.D.) —Paul's sufferings for Christ **Message:** The joy of suffering for Christ	7. Colossians (61-63 A.D.) —the primacy of Christ **Message:** By Him, through Him, for Him	8. 1 Thessalonians (50-52 A.D.) —concern for the new converts —the second coming of Christ **Message:** Christian life is an intense expectation.

9. 2 Thessalonians (50-52 A.D.)	10. 1 Timothy (c 63-64 A.D.)	11. 2 Timothy (65-67 A.D.)
—the second coming of Christ not imminent **Message:** March forward in faith	— advice about Church organization and administration **Message:** In the Church of the living God	—the testament of Paul to Timothy **Message:** I have fought the good fight, I have kept the faith— Come, Lord Jesus.
12. Titus (c. 63-64 A.D.) **Message:** Pastoral advice	13. Philemon (c. 61-63 A.D.) —slave and, now, a brother **Message:** Union of all Christians in Christ	14. Hebrews (late sixties or later still) —the old Covenant and the new **Message:** Perseverance

—and 7 other letters	1. James (before 62 A.D.)
	—advice on Christian life
	Message: Be doers of the Word and not hearers only (1:22).
2. 1 Peter (c. 64-67 A.D.) —encouragement to persecuted Christians **Message:** "You are a chosen race, a royal priesthood..." (2:9).	3. 2 Peter (at the turn of the century) —warning against false teachers **Message:** Remain faithful...the Lord will come again.
4. 1 Epistle of John (before the Gospel of John) —Christ is God's revelation **Message:** Life in God's family	5. 2 Epistle of John (c. 90-100 A.D.) —Christian love and steadfast faith **Message:** Authentic Christian life
6. 3 Epistle of John (c. 90-100 A.D.) —to a gracious friend **Message:** Encouragement	7. Jude (uncertain; c. 90 A.D.) —warning against false teachers **Message:** Fidelity to true teaching

and the book of Revelation (c. the time of Domitian's persecution c. 90-96 A.D.)

—encouragement to persecuted Christians
—written in the apocalyptic style of Daniel

Message:
History has a meaning— God is Lord of history. "In the world you will have tribulation; but be of good cheer, I have overcome the world" (Jn. 16:33).

INDEX

A

Abraham 23, 29f., 32ff., 64, 88, 102, 132, 150, 164f., 201, 206, 208, 217, 235f., 239
Abraham Lincoln 165
Achaz 166
Acts 191, 219
Acts of John 150
Acts of the Apostles 189f., 195, 217f.
Adam 72, 150, 240
adulterous woman 204
Advent 264
adversaries 233
Agur 108
Ahikar 110
Alexander the Great 88
alienation 32f.
all-sufficiency of Christ 242
Amarna letters 110
Amos 68, 151f., 158ff., 166f., 172, 188
Anatoth 138
anawim 82
angelology 83
angels 242, 252
announcement 183, 218
annunciation 202
anointing 66
answers to quizzes 275f.
Antichrist 265f.
Antioch in Syria 209
Antiochus III 121
Antiochus IV 146
Antiochus Epiphanes 148
Antiochus Epiphanes IV 88
apocalyptic 149, 184, 269f.
  books 270
  writers 271
apocryphal infancy gospels 150

apokalyptein 149
apostle 237, 266
Apostle, the 199, 238, 242, 246, 248, 251
  admonitions of 249
  pastoral directives of 249
apostles 90, 100, 192, 195, 216f., 219, 231, 258
  preaching of the 218
apostolate 196
apostolic authority 264
apparitions 205
Appendices 57
ark 65
Ascension 195
"Ascent of Mount Carmel" 116
Asia 219, 246
Asia Minor 246
Assyria 68, 126, 129, 159, 166, 168, 170
Assyrian 166
Assyrians 82, 160
atheism 68f.
atonement 39f.
Augustine, St. 113, 117
author 252, 257
authors
  of New Testament 175, 178
  sacred 184

B

Babylon 68, 70, 75, 93, 129, 139, 141, 143, 145, 170f., 174, 179, 271f.
  destruction of 269
Babylonia 143
Babylonian exile 67
Babylonians 139, 170
ban 55 (See also "herem")

Daughters of St. Paul

In Massachusetts
  50 St. Paul's Avenue, *Boston*, Mass. 02130
  172 Tremont Street, *Boston*, Mass. 02111
In New York
  78 Fort Place, *Staten Island*, N.Y. 10301
  625 East 187th Street, *Bronx*, N.Y. 10458
  525 Main Street, *Buffalo*, N.Y. 14203
In Connecticut
  202 Fairfield Avenue, *Bridgeport*, Conn. 06603
In Ohio
  2105 Ontario St. (at Prospect Ave.), *Cleveland*, Ohio 44115
In Pennsylvania
  1127 South Broad Street, *Philadelphia*, Pa. 19147
In Florida
  2700 Biscayne Blvd., *Miami*, Florida 33137
In Louisiana
  4403 Veterans Memorial Blvd., Metairie,
  New Orleans, La. 70002
  86 Bolton Avenue, *Alexandria*, La. 71301
In Missouri
  203 Tenth St. (at Pine), *St. Louis*, Mo. 63101
In Texas
  114 East Main Plaza, *San Antonio*, Texas 78205
In California
  1570 Fifth Avenue, *San Diego*, Calif. 92101
  278 17th Street, *Oakland*, Calif. 94612
  46 Geary Street, *San Francisco*, Calif. 94108
In Canada
  3022 Dufferin Street, *Toronto* 395, Ontario, Canada
In England
  57, Kensington Church Street, *London* W. 8, England
In Australia
  58, Abbotsford Rd., Homebush, N.S.W., *Sydney* 2140,
  Australia